Master · Classes ™

AL DI MEOLA

a guide to Chords, Scales, & Arpeggios

by AL DI MEOLA & BOB ASLANIAN

Produced by JOHN CERULLO
Cover Art and Design by J.J. FLANNERY
Type Editing by CAROL FLANNERY

Distributed by HAL LEONARD PUBLISHING CORPORATION

BOB ASLANIAN

Bob Aslanian has been playing guitar professionally for thirty years. He has spent a good part of that time teaching the guitar, as well as playing in big bands, small combos, and presently in solo performance. He has recorded two record albums and has worked frequently as a studio musician. He is now living in New Jersey, playing and teaching the guitar.

AL DI MEOLA

Al arrived as a powerful and influential force in music on his own terms, playing a brand of music that cannot be categorized. This blend includes elements of rock, jazz, classical, and Latin rhythms woven into beautiful melodies played on acoustic and electric instruments.

His early training with jazz guitarist Bob Aslanian emphasized reading, picking technique, and technical proficiency, as well as the ability to appreciate and play many types of music. Since that time, Al has had a most successful career. Besides his continuing success as one of the world's greatest solo artists, Al has played with some of today's most talented musicians. From his early days with Barry Miles and Chick Corea's Return To Forever, to his most recent work with the Trio of John McLaughlin, Paco DeLucia, and himself, Al is still growing as an artist. His recent work on solo acoustic guitar is proof of that. He owes much of his past and present success to his taking the time and effort to develop a good base of musical knowledge and theory. Al has said, "by not developing good musical and technical proficiency, a guitarist is not giving himself the chance to become the best that he or she can be. So it is my hope that people will use this book that Bob Aslanian and myself have developed as a tool that will give a person the chance to become a good musician. All one needs to do is work hard."

INTRODUCTION

It is the intention of this book to help you learn some of the chords, scales, and arpeggios necessary in becoming a good musician and player. You can learn these step-by-step, one day at a time, through our unique Lesson Plan System. This System eliminates your having to work through a chord book, a scale book, and an arpeggio book. Instead, it brings all of these elements together in one system, presented in a relatively easy to understand approach.

The different chords, scales, arpeggios, reading tips, chord progressions, exercises, tunes, and supplementary material will give you a complete education, not only in guitar, but in music in general. So think of yourself as a young carpenter learning how to use his tools. This system will give you the tools and then show you how and when to use them in developing your own style and in developing yourself as a well-rounded musician and player.

Over the past twenty years of teaching guitar, the two most common questions asked by new students are: why should I learn all these chords, scales, arpeggios, etc? And, just how is all this going to really help me? To answer both of these questions, we simply ask you to think of yourself as a carpenter's apprentice, learning how and when to use the tools of his trade. Once you have learned this, then you can apply this knowledge in creating, designing, and building whatever you desire.

Our System does the same thing by providing you with the necessary tools of your trade (chords, scales, arpeggios, etc.). Teaching you how, when, and where to use these tools will help you create and build better lead solos and eventually help you develop into a more rounded guitarist and musician.

FOREWORD

As you look through this book, you'll notice one very obvious and different element that you will not see in any other technique book on guitar. This book has been divided into individual sections: Lesson Plans, Chord Section, Scale Section, Arpeggio Section, and Tune and Exercises Section. There is a very important reason for setting up this book in this fashion.

It is our belief that most guitar technique publications are very difficult to work with. They tend to become unclear and out of focus for the student. So we have structured this technique book to have the **10 Lesson Plan** program right in the beginning of the book, clearly laying out exactly what to study, in simple outline fashion.

Our goal is that you can easily follow this program, all the while learning to play guitar with the most solid base of technique available today.

We have included in the back of this book a list of publications we believe will help enhance your technical ability because we believe that no one book, including this one, can cover the complete scope of guitar technique. We have devised a unique feature in this book by also listing some of these supplemental publications precisely at the right place and time inside of each **Lesson Plan.**

CONTENTS

WARM-UP AND DEVELOPING SPEED EXERCISES

We feel that one of the best ways to warm up and develop speed is to practice using scale exercises. We suggest you start by using the Major Scale and using either the A or B fingering. Use the alternate picking technique (down-up stroke pattern) and begin with a slow tempo. Practice the scale, first in eighth notes, then in eighth note triplets, sixteenth notes, and in broken thirds, ascending and descending in two octaves. Once you feel comfortable playing this scale at a slow tempo, then gradually pick up the tempo and repeat the entire exercise. After working with fingerings A and B, we suggest repeating the entire exercise using fingerings C, D, and E. These fingerings are great for stretching your fingers.

There are several things to remember. First, the warm up exercises should total no more than fifteen to twenty minutes at the beginning of each practice session. Train, don't strain. Second, always begin the exercise with a slow tempo and don't increase the tempo until you can play the scale smoothly.

Over the years, guitar players have used certain tricks to help strengthen their fingers and develop speed. As crazy as they may seem, they do work. The first trick is to practice all scale fingerings wearing a tight rubber glove on your left hand. Another trick is to use very heavy gauge strings and raise the action on your guitar a little higher than usual. When playing scales or arpeggios, remember to keep the fingers of your left hand as close to the strings as possible. This is not only proper technique, but a little trick in developing speed. The greater the distance your fingers have to travel to hold down a string, time will be wasted, thus losing speed.

GOOD PRACTICE HABITS

We feel that developing good practice habits is essential not only in helping you learn how to play properly, but in helping you quickly advance and reach your ultimate goal, becoming a master guitarist and musician.

The first thing we would like to discuss is how to hold the instrument. The proper way to hold the guitar when practicing, is to sit on a chair or stool with both feet flat on the floor, and have the body of the guitar rest on your right leg. In order to have a clear view of the entire fingerboard and be comfortable, it will be necessary to angle the body of the guitar just enough to allow you to lean slightly forward over the body.

It is perfectly all right to wear a guitar strap of your choice if it keeps your guitar from sliding around on your leg, however it is certainly not a requirement.

We strongly advise using a good music stand. We do not recommend placing your music on a bed, on the floor, or on a table because it not only makes reading music difficult, but could damage your eyes. In addition, it also makes it harder to hold your guitar properly as we described above.

Purchasing and using a good metronome when practicing your lessons will definitely be quite helpful in developing a strong feel for timing.

We also suggest learning how to keep time by tapping with your left foot.

In order to quickly advance, each power packed **Lesson Plan** in this system will require seriously practicing every day. Since each practice session will require total concentration, a quiet place to practice will be important.

How long should you practice each day? Initially, to begin with, we suggest practicing each section approximately twenty to forty-five minutes each day. As time goes on, it will be up to you to decide which section of each **Lesson Plan** will need more or less time. Try to increase your total practice time, if you can, to as much as your own personal schedule permits.

When practicing the scales and arpeggios, it is very important not to overpractice and strain your arms and hands. Remember, just like weight lifting, train, don't strain. If you find yourself practicing an exercise over and over again and becoming frustrated with it, we recommend stopping, and either moving on to another exercise or putting the guitar down and walking out of the room. Sometimes giving yourself a couple of hours or even twenty-four hours away from practicing will help you forget your frustrations and help you clear your mind and begin with a fresh outlook on practicing.

We recommend developing good eating, sleeping, and physical exercise habits because the daily concentrated practice sessions will drain your energy both mentally and physically. It is important to remember, as a musician, you must play in smoke filled places and keep late hours. In order to perform four or five hours each night at peak level, you must be in excellent mental and physical condition. Also, sometimes the reason you might find it hard to sit down and practice is because you are not in good overall condition. Practicing takes a lot of everything you've got, so if you want to be successful at learning the guitar, try to develop good practice and overall habits in your life.

As we mentioned earlier, these Lesson Plans are a guide to helping you organize each of your daily practice sessions and develop good practice habits. Each individual Lesson Plan should take approximately two weeks with an average of two hours work per day. Your own practice habits and/or schedule may vary, and everyone should work at his own speed, so use this as a **guide only** in making your own personal schedule and time frame for completing each one of the Lesson Plans. Basically work at your own speed and know that you are doing great if you can complete each Lesson Plan in a two week period. The most important thing is to take your time; make sure you thoroughly understand each step before moving on. Good Luck. . .

PICKING TECHNIQUE

One of the biggest problems students have is choosing a good picking technique. It is obvious that without developing the proper picking technique, the chances of ever developing speed and articulation would be almost impossible. Therefore, we've chosen three excellent techniques to highlight for you: picking from the elbow, from the wrist, and rotating the forefinger and thumb.

Before discussing these techniques, the first thing we would like to cover is finding the right pick. This, we feel, is up to the individual's own taste. We recommend using a heavy gauge pick, but experimenting with all gauges (thin, medium, and heavy) would certainly be a good idea.

Holding the pick is the next important thing we would like to cover. This is simple because there is only one proper way to hold the pick, and that is between the forefinger and the thumb. Any other way is incorrect.

There are three basic picking techniques: picking from the elbow, picking from the wrist, and picking using the forefinger and thumb. It is very important to choose **one** or a **combination** of these techniques before attempting to practice the scale fingerings or arpeggio fingerings. Make sure to try each technique, and then choose the one which feels the most comfortable to you. **Remember**, developing a good picking technique is the **key** to **developing speed and articulation** when playing rhythm chords, chord/melody, scales, and arpeggios.

The first technique we would like to discuss is picking from the elbow. First, hold the pick between your forefinger and your thumb. Keep your wrist straight so your arm and wrist look like one straight line from your elbow to your fingers. We suggest that your arm and hand should **not** touch the guitar. Now, keeping the pick stiff, move your arm up and down **pivoting** from the elbow.

The second technique is picking from the wrist. Holding the pick firmly between your forefinger and thumb, move your hand up and down **pivoting** from the **wrist**. You may rest your elbow on the guitar.

The third technique is picking from the forefinger and thumb. Hold the pick firmly between your forefinger and thumb. You may rest your hand or just a couple of fingers on the pickguard as a guide or support. Now, rotate the pick in **almost a circular motion**, just using your **forefinger and thumb**, keeping your arm and hand straight. Remember, all the picking motion will come from your forefinger and thumb.

Picking From The Elbow

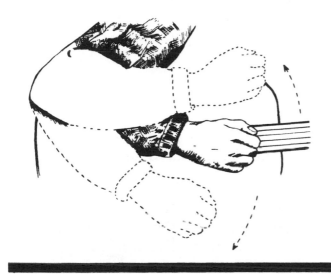

Picking From The Wrist

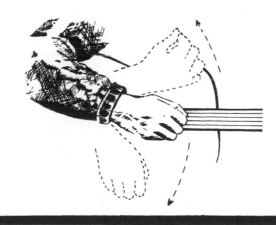

Picking From The Forefinger And Thumb

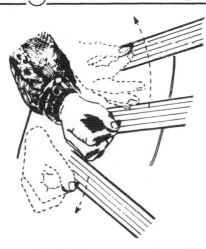

LESSON PLAN ONE

As you can see in the Chord Section, there are ten forms spread out over every two pages. (Turn to the Chord Section and note.) These are the basic chord Forms that you will be learning over the course of this entire system. We will start by learning one Form at a time.

Step #1

Start by memorizing all the Form I chords on page 24. Strum each chord four times using a simple down strum and be able to switch smoothly from G to GMaj7, to G7, to GMaj6. The square note on the sixth string, third fret, is the chord root (or chord name note). This is your guide note. It will help you move to other frets along the sixth string while keeping this Form I chord position in place. You create the same four chords except in different positions with a new root name. An example of this would be to move the four chords in Form I up to the V position. The root note on the sixth string, fifth fret, is A. These four chords would now be A, AMaj7, A7, AMaj6. Practice the four Form I chords by starting from the first fret, sixth string, which is F, memorizing the chord name in that position. Then move up one fret to F# or Gb and practice switching the chords (strum each one four times) while memorizing their names in that position. Repeat this same procedure moving one fret higher each time. Remember, before moving to the next higher position, you must be able to switch the chords smoothly and know them by their chord names and frets.

Step #2

Once you have memorized the Form I, G, GMaj7, G7, GMaj6 in all positions, turn to page 26 and repeat the same practice procedure with Form I, Gm, GmM7, Gm7, Gm6. Remember to follow the sixth string root. Start at the first fret and work your way up the fretboard one position at a time, learning to play these chords while memorizing the chord names and fret positions.

Step #3

Turn to page 28 and follow the same procedure of learning all four chords in Form I, GMaj7, GMaj9, Gm9, G6/9.

Step #4

Turn now to page 30 where you'll find Form I, G7, G9, G7(b9), G7(#9). Make sure to practice these chords by following the same procedures as in the previous step.

Step #5

Turn to page 32 and find the diminished chords. Unlike previous chords in Form I, there is only one chord switch to make here, G7 to Gdim.

Important Note: Any note in a diminished chord may be considered the **root.** In this system we are keeping the root as the lowest note in this chord. The diminished chords repeat themselves (the notes of the chord being inverted) every four frets.

Step #6

Turn to page 34 and practice Form I, G7, G7(b5), G7(#5).

Step #7

Turn to page 36 and practice Form I, GMaj7, GMaj7(#5), GMaj7(b5), Gm7(b5). Make sure to continue following the previous procedure when practicing these chords. Remember to learn the chord names and fret positions.

Step #8

Turn to page 38 and memorize Form I, G7, G7sus4, Gm11, G9(+11).

Step #9

Turn now to page 40 and memorize Form I, G13, G13(b9), G13(#9). Follow the same procedure as in all previous steps.

Step #10

Turn to page 80 to the **Jazz Chord Exercise Studies I** and memorize exercise I. Once this has been memorized, practice this exercise in other positions, just as we learned the different chord Forms in different positions.

Step #11

We now take you to page 85 for the **12 Bar Blues** chord patterns. Please read the introduction to this section on page 84 before you start. Practice playing exercises I, II, and III, memorizing each pattern. Once you have done this, try these 12 Bar Blues patterns in other positions and memorize them as well.

Step #12

Turn to page 42 and read the introduction to the **Scale Section.** After reading the introduction, turn to page 43 and you will find the Form I, A Major Scale written out with five different fingerings all starting on the 5th fret, sixth string root. Begin by memorizing the A and B fingerings of the A Major Scale. Make sure to use the right fingerings and to read the notes on the staff. Always know what note you are playing and where it is on the fingerboard as you go along in the scale.

Practice these two scales as shown in the Major Scale exercises, which you will find on page 46. These exercises will help you to learn how to read and play in the most commonly used rhythm patterns. These exercises are written out for you in fingering pattern A. Practice these exercises with fingering pattern B as well. Once you have done this, learn to play these scale fingerings A and B in other positions, as you did with the chords in Form I, using the sixth string as your root.

Step #13

Now turn to page 62 and read the introduction to the Arpeggio Section. Turn to page 63 and memorize the fingerings A, B, and C to the A Major and A minor arpeggios.

Remember, these Form I fingerings once again have a sixth string root, so once you have memorized these arpeggios, you can practice them in other positions working from the sixth string root.

Make sure to practice playing each arpeggio ascending and descending all in smooth and fluid eighth notes.

LESSON PLAN TWO

Steps #1-9

Turn to the Chord Section, pages 24 thru 41, and start memorizing **all** the chord fingerings in **Form II**, following the same practice procedure as in Lesson One. Be able to switch smoothly from C, to CMaj7, to C7, to CMaj6. Remember, the Form II chords have a **fifth string root**. Once you have memorized the Form II chord fingerings and their names, start from the first fret, fifth string, which is Bb, and work these four chords in each position, moving up the fingerboard one fret higher each time.

Step #10

We now turn to page 80 and practice exercises II, III, IV, and V in the **Jazz Chord Exercise Studies I** sheet.

Strumming Tip: With any of the exercises or tunes in this book, for practice purposes, remember to use a **simple down strum** for each beat of the measure. What is important right now is to be able to switch chord changes smoothly, while memorizing their names and their positions.

Important Note: Once you have completed memorizing the Form II chords on all the pages in the Chord Section, we suggest testing yourself by playing any chord in two different positions.

EXAMPLE: (FMaj7) would be played at the (first fret) sixth string root, (FMaj7) would be played at the (eighth fret) fifth string root, (Gm7) would be played at the (third fret) sixth string root, and (Gm7) would be played at the (tenth fret) fifth string root.

As you move on to the other chord Forms, you will be learning how to play each chord ten different ways. We have found that most guitar players generally have three or four "pet" chord Forms for every chord. As you go through this System, you will have the opportunity to choose your favorite chord Forms, but of course if you can use all ten chord Forms, that is even better.

Remember, when playing rhythm chords in an actual band situation, you will want to keep your chords close together and avoid large leaps. If you jump all over the fingerboard, the chances of a mistake will be greater. Also, generally speaking, the best chordal sounding range of the guitar falls between the first fret and the eighth fret. Again we are talking strictly about rhythm chord accompaniment. You will also notice that most of the chords in this system are not six string chords. That means that you should learn to strum only the notes that are marked in each chord Form and nothing more. As we move along, you will learn that it is not necessary to play more than a three or four tone chord. There are certain notes in a chord that are more important to play than others. Usually, the least important tones are the root and perfect 5th. The 3rd and the 7th are the most important. We strongly suggest picking up a good book on music theory to help you understand some of the terms mentioned in this system. We want to state clearly that this system is not a text on theory.

Step #11

Turn to page 86 and begin to memorize exercises IV and V in the **12 Bar Blues** chord patterns. Once you have mastered these exercises, memorize these 12 Bar Blues in other positions.

Step #12

Now turn to page 43 to the Major Scales and memorize fingerings C and D. Practice these two scale fingerings along with the A and B fingerings, ascending (going up) and descending (going down) in eighth notes, eighth note triplets, broken thirds, and sixteenth notes. Examples of these rhythmic patterns are on page 46.

Now turn to pages 48 and 49, and work each scale fingering pattern as shown.

Step #13

Turn to page 63 and memorize the fingerings A, B, C, and Form I of the AMaj7 and AminMaj7 arpeggios. These arpeggio fingerings should be mastered in every position, ascending and descending in eighth notes.

LESSON PLAN THREE

Steps #1-9

Memorize **all** the **chords** in Form III. Repeat steps #1-9 as in Lesson Plan One and Lesson Plan Two. Start on page 24 working through to page 41.

Step #10

Memorize exercise VI and VII on the **Jazz Chord Exercise Studies I** sheet on page 81.

Step #11

Memorize the **12 Bar Blues** patterns VI & VII starting on page 87. Again, memorize these patterns in every position.

If you have been keeping up with your Lesson Plans, you should be able to play both the **basic chords** and **chord substitutions** without much trouble. If you have any problems, we suggest going back to Lesson Plans One and Two and reviewing them.

Remember, the strumming technique is a simple down strum for every beat of the measure. As you play through the chord changes, pay special attention to chord substitutions and their application. The chord substitutions really begin to set up the chord substitutions for the rest of the tunes in this section. On page 109 you will find a handy **Master Guide For Basic Chord Substitutions,** which might also help you understand and memorize these substitutions.

Step #12

Turn to page 44 and memorize fingering E, Form I, A Major Scale and follow the same practice procedure as in Step #12, Lesson Plan Two.

Step #13

Turn to page 63 and memorize fingerings A, B, and C, A7, Am7, arpeggios. Again, these fingerings must be memorized in every position.

Now turn to page 65 to the Form I Arpeggio Studies I. Exercises A, B, and C on this page must be practiced and memorized in all positions ascending and descending as written.

LESSON PLAN FOUR

Steps #1-9

Memorize the fingerings of all the chords in Form IV, on pages 24 through 41.

Step #10

Turn to page 81 and memorize exercises VIII, IX, and X in the **Jazz Chord Studies I.**

Step #11

Pick up the Bugs Bower **Rhythm Book** Volume I and II and begin to sight-read all the exercises on the first four pages in the various positions, as mentioned in Lesson Plan Three, Step #11. Do not memorize these exercises or you will be defeating the purpose of sight-reading.

Sight-Reading Tip: First choose the right position for each exercise, and without playing, try to count out the rhythmic pattern for each measure. Then go back and play the exercise. Begin practicing slowly, gradually trying to increase the tempo. We suggest going through each eight bar exercise three to four times per night.

Step #12

Turn to page 88 and memorize the **12 Bar Blues** pattern VIII. Again, memorize this pattern in every position. Next, turn to page 92 and learn the chord changes to the tune "Ritmo De La Noche." Transpose and learn in other positions.

Once the chord changes in this tune have been mastered, begin to read the melody. We suggest learning to read all the tunes in this System and in any of the Suggested Supplementary Materials in several positions.

If you are weak with your reading, we suggest that you pick up any of the various beginners' books and review all of your notes.

Step #13

Turn to page 70 and begin to memorize the fingerings A, B, C, Form II, D Major and D minor arpeggio. Remember to practice and memorize these fingerings ascending and descending in every position.

Step #14

Turn to page 64 and memorize fingerings A, B, C, Form I, A7(b5) and Am7(b5) arpeggios. Memorize these in every position, ascending and descending.

Now turn to pages 66 & 67 and work on Form I Arpeggio Studies II and III.

LESSON PLAN FIVE

Steps #1-9

Memorize all the chord fingerings of Form V (pages 24 thru 41).

Step #10

Practice and work out both the chords and melody to "Dinner Music Of The Gods" on page 95. Also, try "Al Di's Dream Theme" on page 100. Practice both the chords and melodies in different positions.

Step #11

Turn to page 82 and memorize exercises I and II in the **Jazz Chord Studies II.**

Step #12

Practice the exercise on the next six pages of the Bug Bower books.

Step #13

Get a copy of **Classical Studies for Pick-Style Guitar,** and begin to practice the first piece, "Caprice." This book will not only introduce you to some good classical pieces, but it will also help further improve your picking technique and reading skills. We suggest going slowly and mastering each piece, one at a time. There will be no time limit for completing each piece in this book.

Step #14

Turn to pages 52 & 53 and memorize all the fingerings of both Form I, A minor, Pure Scale and Form II, D minor, Pure Scale. All these fingerings will be practiced and memorized in every position, ascending and descending, in eighth notes, eighth note triplets, broken thirds, and sixteenth notes.

Step #15

Memorize the fingerings for A7(#5) and Adim7 arpeggios Form I (page 64).

Turn to pages 68 & 69 and practice exercises 4 and 5 on the Form I Arpeggio Study sheets. Again, all three exercises on each sheet must be completed and practiced in every position.

LESSON PLAN SIX

Step #1-9

Go to the Chord Section and memorize all the chord fingerings to Form VI (pages 24 thru 41).

Step #10

Turn to page 89 in the **12 Bar Blues** section, and practice and memorize the chords to patterns IX and X. Practice in every position.

Step #11

Turn to page 82 and memorize exercise III and IV in the **Jazz Chord Studies II.**

Step #12

Practice the next six pages in Bugs Bower's book. From this point on, we suggest taking six to eight pages in this book every two weeks.

Step #13

Pick up the book **Melodic Rhythms** by William Leavitt and begin practicing the chords and melodies to the first three exercises. Once you have mastered these exercises, we suggest averaging four exercises per two week practice period.

This book will help improve your knowledge of the use of chords, chord progressions, chord turn-arounds, and it will help improve your ability to sight-read.

Step #14

Turn to pages 54 and 55. Practice and memorize all the fingerings to both A minor Harmonic Scale Form I and D minor Harmonic Scale Form II.

Step #15

Turn to page 64 in the Arpeggio Section and memorize all the fingerings for the AMaj6 and Amin6 arpeggios Form I.

Now go to page 69 and memorize exercises 6 and 7 in the Form I Arpeggio Studies.

LESSON PLAN SEVEN

Steps #1-9

Practice and memorize all fingerings to the Form VII chords (pages 24 thru 41).

Step #10

Turn to page 90 and memorize the 12 Bar Blues exercise XI.

Step #11

Turn to page 82 and memorize exercises V and VI in the **Jazz Chord Studies II**.

Step #12

Turn to pages 56 and 57. Practice and memorize all the fingerings to both the A Jazz Melodic Minor Scale and the D Jazz Melodic Minor Scale, Form I.

Step #13

Turn to page 70. Practice and memorize, in all positions, the fingerings to DMaj7 and Dmin/Maj7, Form II.

LESSON PLAN EIGHT

Steps #1-9

Memorize all fingerings of chords in Form VIII (pages 24 thru 41).

Step #10

Turn to the Tune Section and practice the chords and melody to "Lady Of Rome, Sister Of Brazil." Try playing both the chords and melody in different positions.

Step #11

Turn to page 83 and memorize exercises VII and VIII in the **Jazz Chord Studies II.**

Step #12

Turn to page 50 and memorize all the fingerings of the Modes. Be sure to read the important footnote on page 51 explaining how the Modes are built.

Step #13

Now turn to pages 70 and 71. Memorize and practice the fingerings to D7, Dm7, D7(b5), and Dm7(b5) arpeggios, Form II, in every position.

Turn to pages 72, 73, & 74. Practice exercise A, B, and C of Form II Arpeggio Studies 1, 2, and 3.

LESSON PLAN NINE

Steps #1-9

Memorize all fingerings to the Form IX chords (pages 24 thru 41).

Step #10

Memorize the chords to exercise XII of the **12 Bar Blues** patterns on page 90. Learn in other positions.

Step #11

Memorize exercises IX and X in the Jazz Chord Exercises II on page 83.

The chords and melodies to all the tunes should be coming to you a little more easily by now. If you are having any problems with the chords or the melodies, we suggest going back and reviewing those sections.

Step #12

Turn to page 47. Memorize all the fingerings of the Pentatonic Scale.

The Chromatic, Minor, and Funky minor Pentatonic Scales will probably sound more familiar to you than the other scales you have been learning up till now. These three scales are the most popular scales used for rock and blues improvisation. Many leads are built from these scales by using either the entire scale or just a few notes from the scale and making up some simple blues licks.

Once you have mastered the fingerings to all the Pentatonic Scales, turn back to the 12 Bar Blues exercises II, III, and IV, and see if you hear the MINOR, Chromatic, and Funky minor scales over the chord changes. This is really the beginning of improvisation.

A Tip On Blues Improvisation: One of the reasons why rock and blues lead players use the Minor, Chromatic, Funky minor Pentatonic Scales is because one scale will sound right over **all** the 12 Bar Blues progression. An example would be playing a G Funky minor Pentatonic Scale over G7, C7, and D9 chords in the 12 Bar Blues exercise II. Remember, you don't have to keep playing the entire scale. You can use just a few notes from the scale. The more you keep practicing with these three scales, the more you'll start to hear how they fit. As we mentioned before, listen to your favorite artists and hear how they phrase their leads. Listen, experiment, and then listen, experiment, and practice some more. This is not something that is going to come to you overnight. Be patient.

Step #13

Turn to page 71. Practice and memorize all the fingerings of D7(#5), Ddim7, DMaj7, and Dm6 arpeggios, Form II. Once again, as in previous lessons, these fingerings should be memorized ascending and descending in every position.

Step #14

Turn to page 75 and practice and memorize exercises 4 and 5 in the Arpeggio Studies, Form II.

LESSON PLAN TEN

Steps #1-9

Complete all the fingerings of Form X in the Chord Section (pages 24 through 41).

Step #10

Memorize exercise XI and XII in the Jazz Chord Exercises II on page 83.

Step #11

Memorize the chords to exercise XIII of the 12 Bar Blues on page 91.

Step #12

Memorize the fingerings to all the Diminished Scales on pages 58 and 59.

Step #13

Turn to pages 60 and 61. Begin practicing and memorizing the fingerings to the Whole Tone Scales.

Step #14

Turn to pages 77 and 78 and complete exercises 6 and 7 in the Form II Arpeggio Studies.

Step #15

Turn back to the first tune in the **Al Di Meola Tunes Section.** Beginning with this tune, look over the Master Guide chart for Chord/Scale relationships starting on page 106 and the Master Guide Chart for Chord/Arpeggio relationships on page 108. Begin trying to improvise over the basic chords, first by experimenting with the scales and modes, then the arpeggios. Once you feel comfortable improvising over the chord changes to this first tune, pick the next tune and go on from there. You can do this with the **12 Bar Blues pattern as well.**

CHORD SECTION

There is a reason for setting up this System with the Chord Section first. In addition, the Chord Section is laid out in a certain fashion for good reason, which you'll understand as we go along.

First, we must realize that some fifty to sixty years ago the guitar was used as a **rhythm instrument** and that it emerged as a **solo instrument** in the early forties. So it was and will always be considered first a rhythm instrument, second a solo instrument. Developing a good chordal foundation will be necessary in becoming a good rhythm player and providing the basis for the creation of solo playing as well. No matter what type of style you are soloing in, jazz, fusion, rock, pop, etc., you are constantly working in the context of the chordal harmony of the tune.

In order to become a good musician and player, you must first start by developing a good solid chord vocabulary. The Chord Section in this book will help you create and develop this vocabulary.

Important Note: Before moving on and beginning the study program in this book, we feel that we must first define a well-rounded musician and a well-rounded player. They are not necessarily the same. A well-rounded musician is one who can read music, has a good working knowledge of music theory, chords, scales, arpeggios and is able to play all styles of music: rock, jazz, fusion, and classical. In other words, he has to know it all. The well-rounded player can play well, but he doesn't necessarily know what he is doing because of a lack of knowledge of theory. A good player is generally self-taught and does not know how to read music or have a good working knowledge of chords, scales, and arpeggios. He relies on his ability to hear certain chord changes and his natural talent for playing leads that he feels sound correct.

Chord Voicing

CHORD VOICING — The notes that make up a chord are referred to as voicings. For now, the two basic voicings we are interested in are the root or bass note (generally the lowest note in the chord) and the lead or soprano voicing (or the highest note of the chord). These two voicings are important when playing chords because they should be moving in various cycles. (Chromatic Cycle, Cycle of 4ths, Cycle of 5ths, Cycle of flatted 5ths, etc.)

EXAMPLE: chord progression Am7 — D7(b9) — GM7.
The A note in an Am7 Form I chord is the root or bass voicing. The E note in an Am7 Form I chord is the lead or soprano voicing. As this chord progresses to the D7(b9) Form II, the A moves upward in a cycle of 4ths to D, the root in a D7(b9). The E moves chromatically lower to Eb, which is the flat 9th of the D7(b9) chord or the lead voicing. As the D7(b9) progresses to the GM7 chord, Form I, the D in the D7(b9) chord moves in an upward cycle of 4ths to G, the root or bass note of the GM7 chord. The Eb in the D7(b9) chord moves chromatically lower to a D, which is the lead or soprano note of the GM7 chord.

So as you work on the different exercises and tunes throughout this book or any of the other supplementary material, try to pick out the cycle movement and learn to apply them in your own personal musical situation.

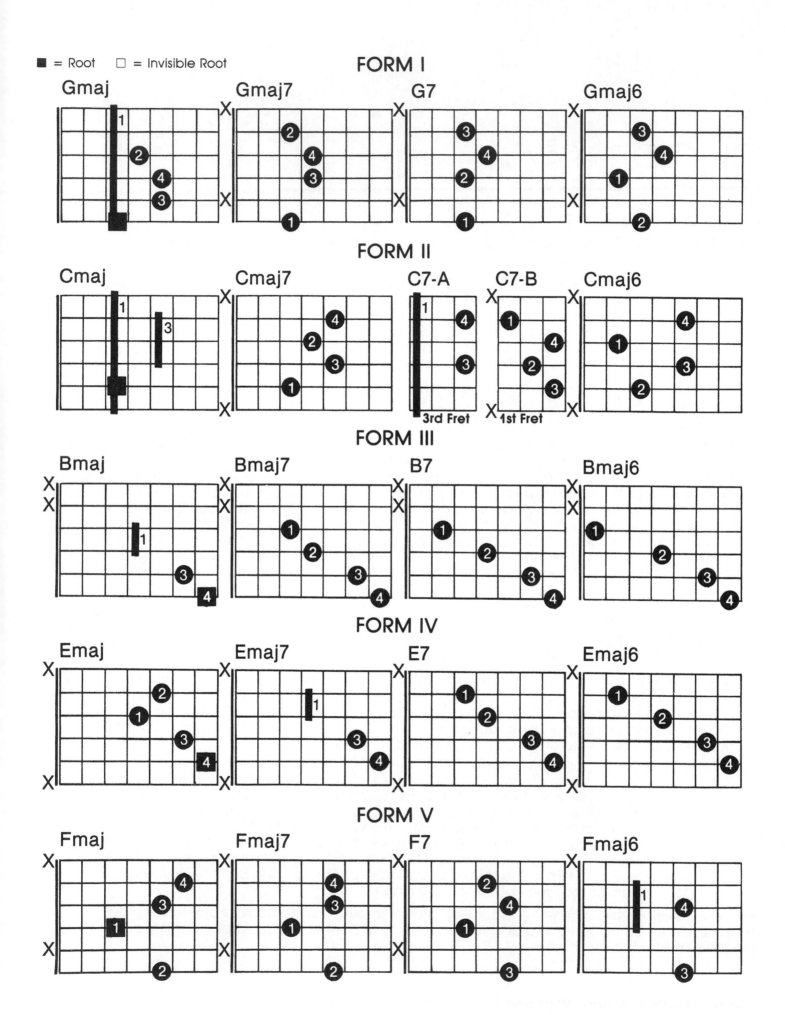

■ = Root   □ = Invisible Root

FORM I

Gmaj   Gmaj7   G7   Gmaj6

FORM II

Cmaj   Cmaj7   C7-A   C7-B   Cmaj6

3rd Fret   1st Fret

FORM III

Bmaj   Bmaj7   B7   Bmaj6

FORM IV

Emaj   Emaj7   E7   Emaj6

FORM V

Fmaj   Fmaj7   F7   Fmaj6

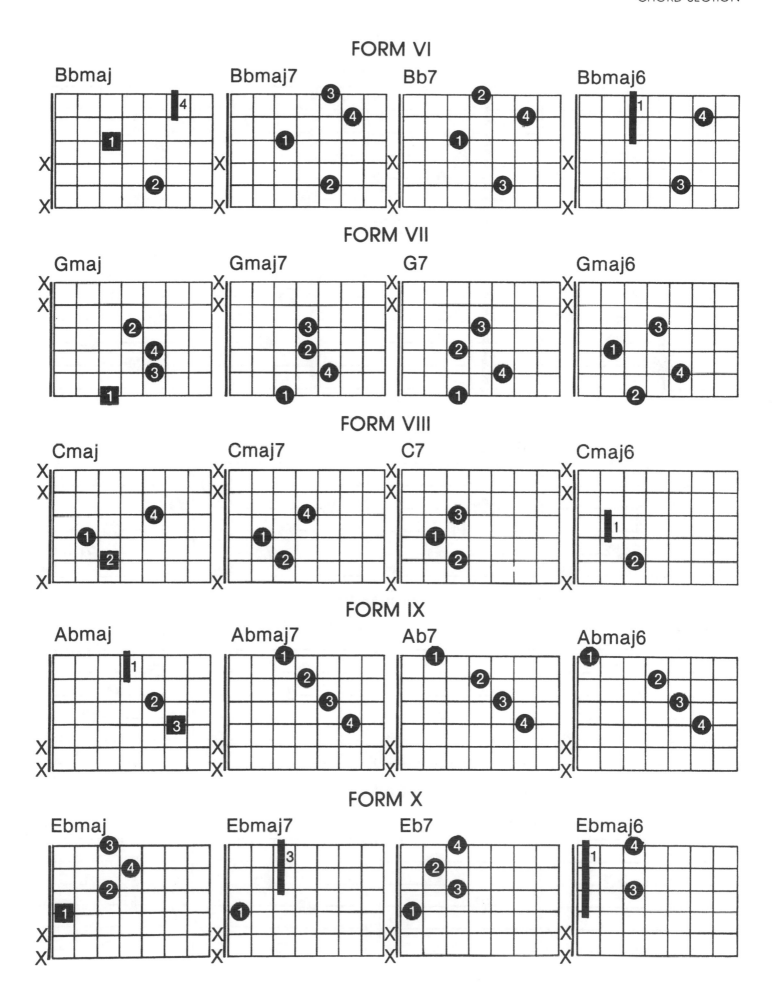

FORM I

Gm   Gm/maj7   Gm7   Gm6

FORM II

Cm   Cm/maj7   Cm7   Cm6

FORM III

Bm   Bm/maj7   Bm7   Bm6

FORM IV

Em   Em/maj7   Em7   Em6

FORM V

Fm   Fm/maj7   Fm7   Fm6

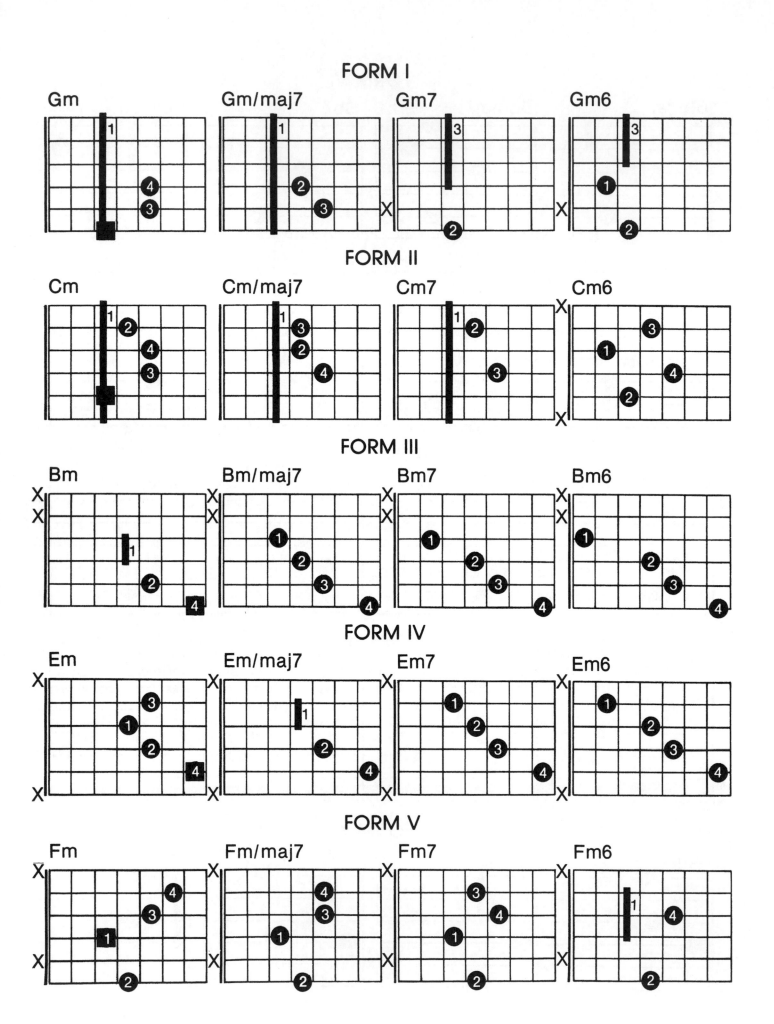

26

FORM VI

Bbm Bbm/maj7 Bbm7 Bbm6

FORM VII

Gm Gm/maj7 Gm7 Gm6

FORM VIII

Cm Cm/maj7 Cm7 Cm6

FORM IX

Abm Abm/maj7 Abm7 Abm6

FORM X

Ebm Ebm/maj7 Ebm7 Ebm6

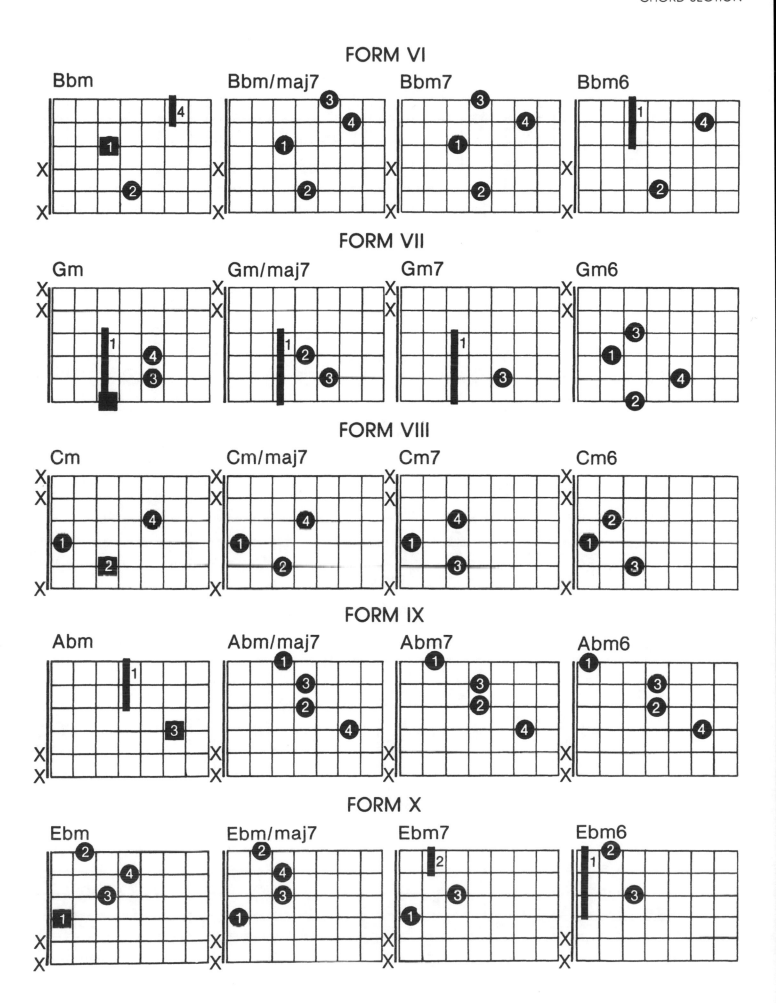

FORM I

Gmaj7 Gmaj9 Gm9 Gmaj6/9

FORM II

Cmaj7 Cmaj9 Cm9 Cmaj6/9

FORM III

Bmaj7 Bmaj9 Bm9 Bmaj6/9

FORM IV

Emaj7 Emaj9 Em9 Emaj6/9

FORM V

Fmaj7 Fmaj9 Fm9 Fmaj6/9

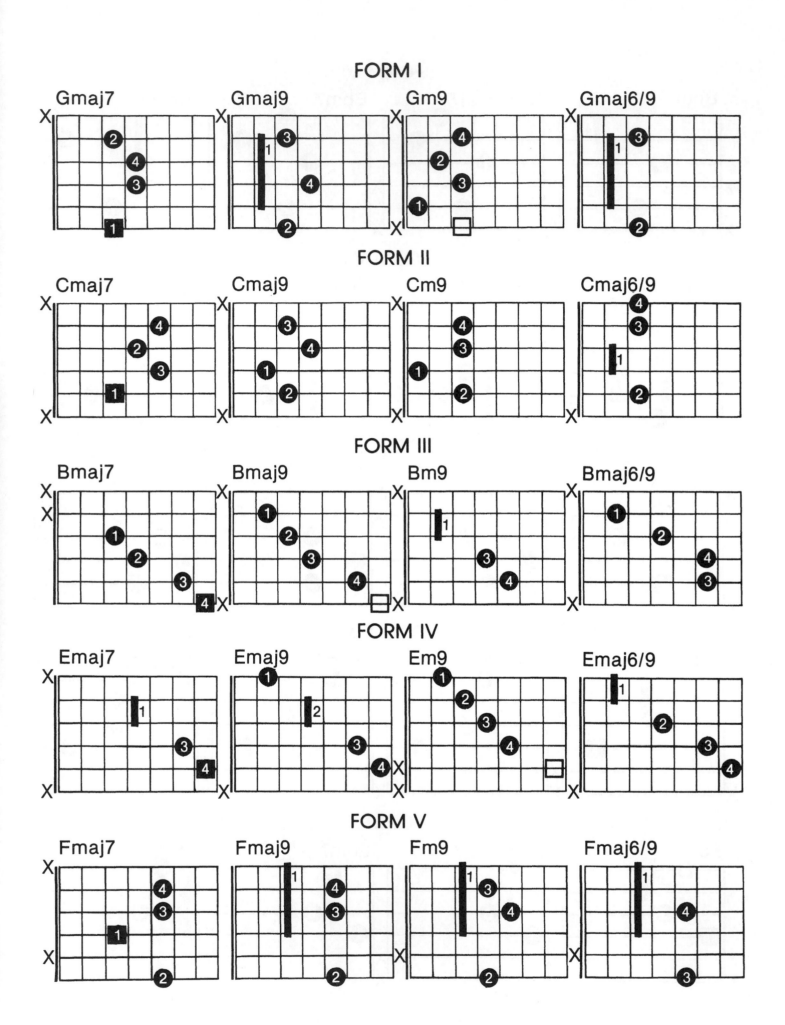

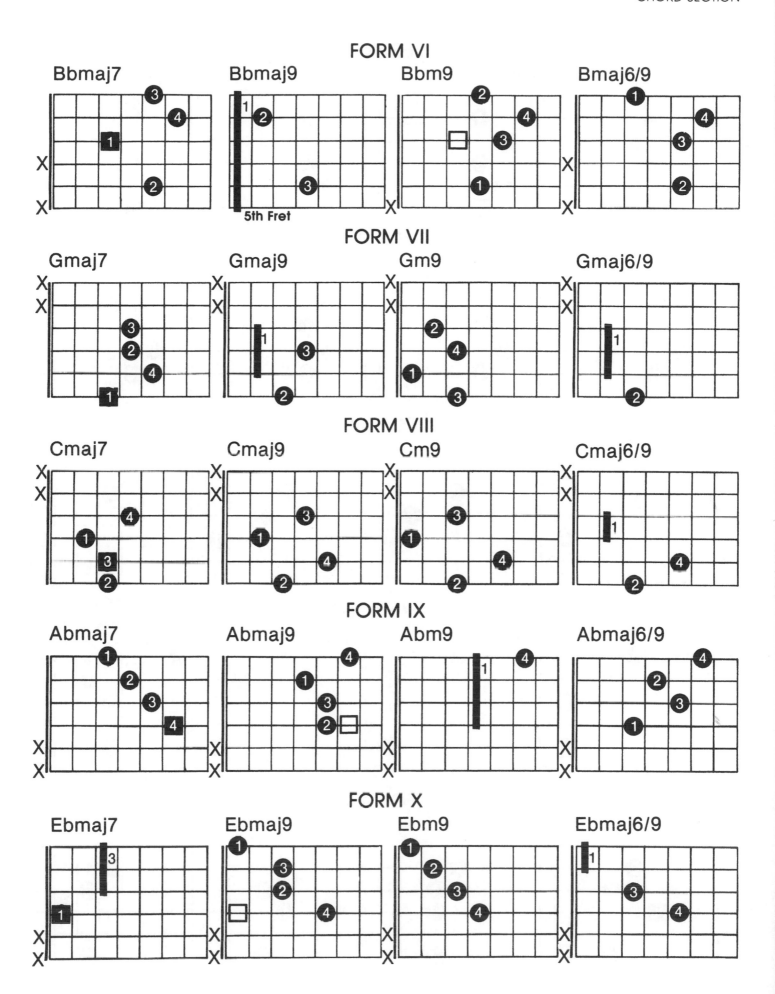

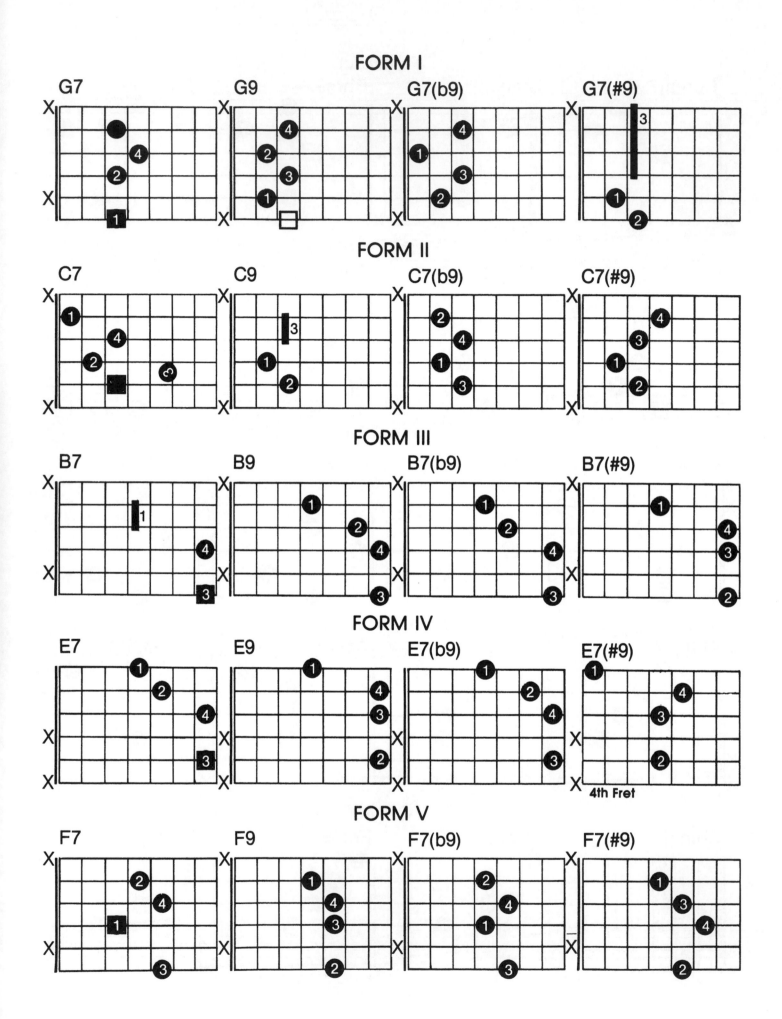

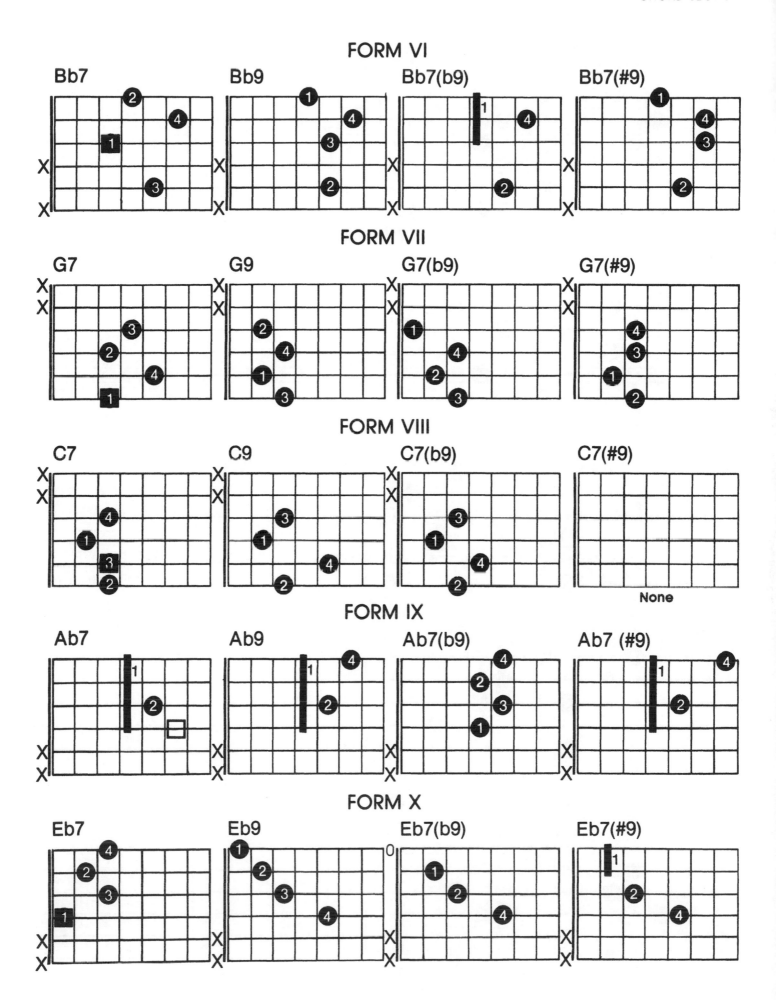

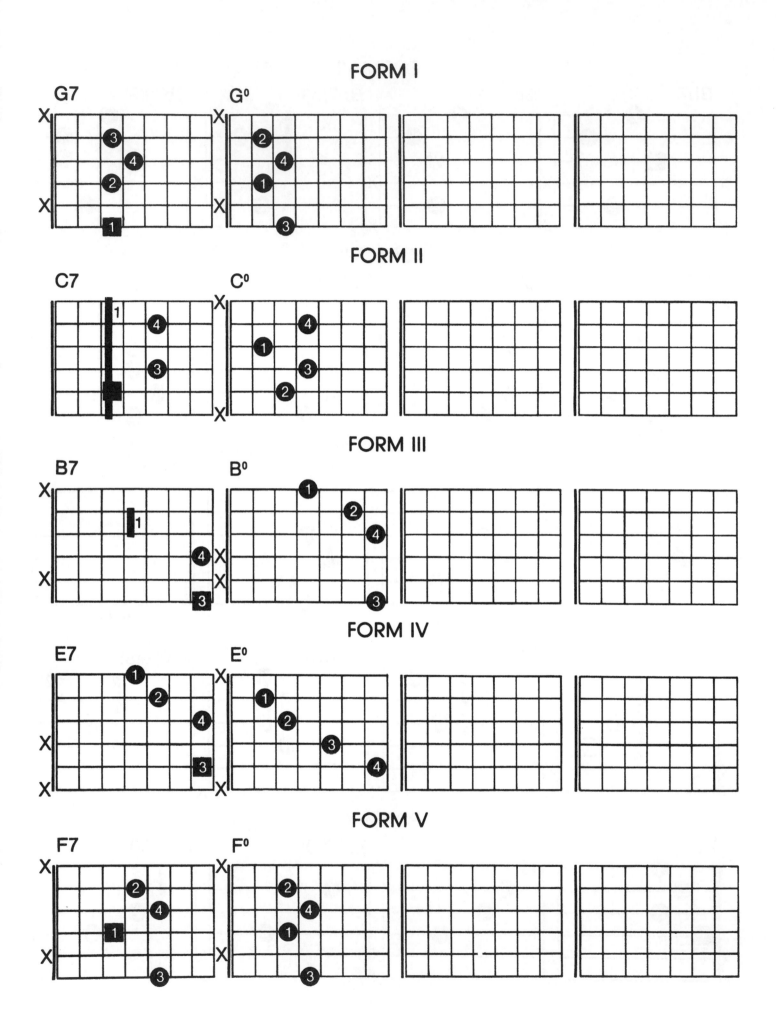

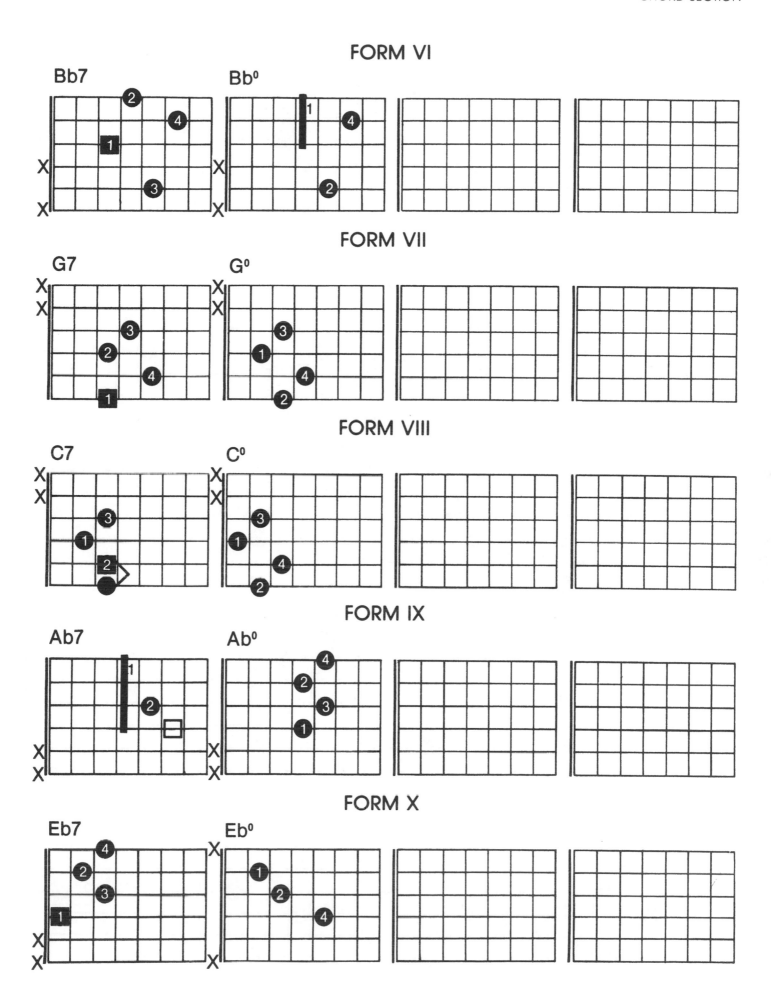

FORM VI

Bb7   Bb⁰

FORM VII

G7   G⁰

FORM VIII

C7   C⁰

FORM IX

Ab7   Ab⁰

FORM X

Eb7   Eb⁰

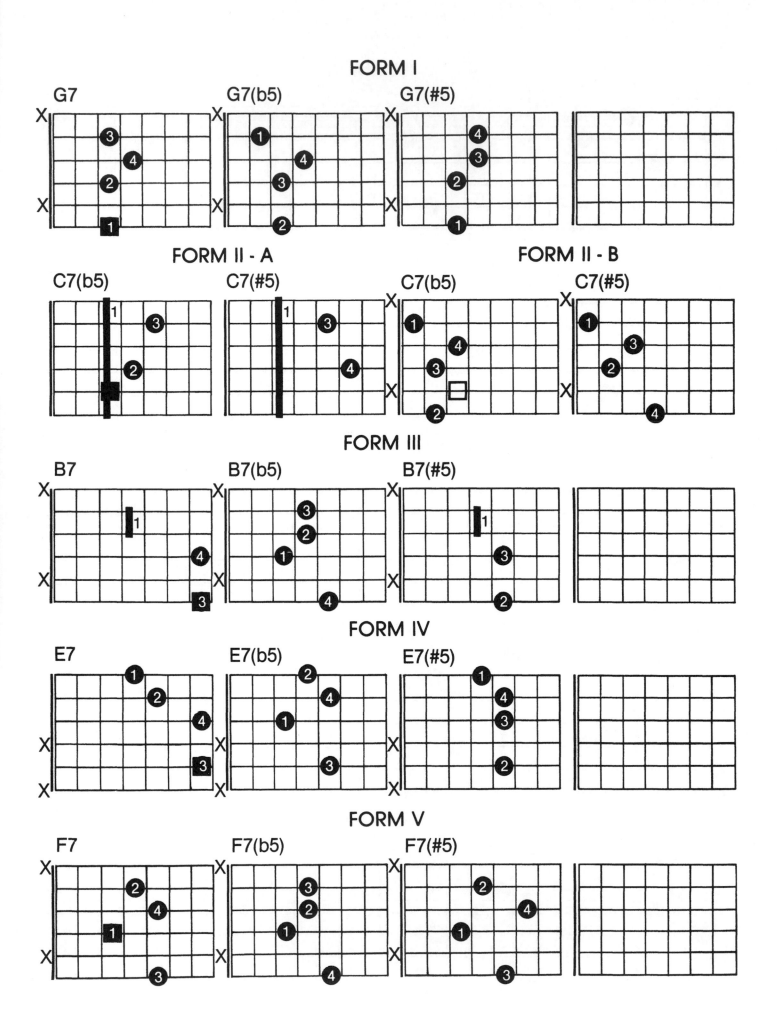

FORM VI

Bb7 Bb7(b5) Bb7(#5)

FORM VII

G7 G7(b5) G7(#5)

FORM VIII

C7 C7(b5) C7(#5)

FORM IX

Ab7 Ab7(b5) Ab7(#5)

FORM X

Eb7 Eb7(b5) Eb7(#5)

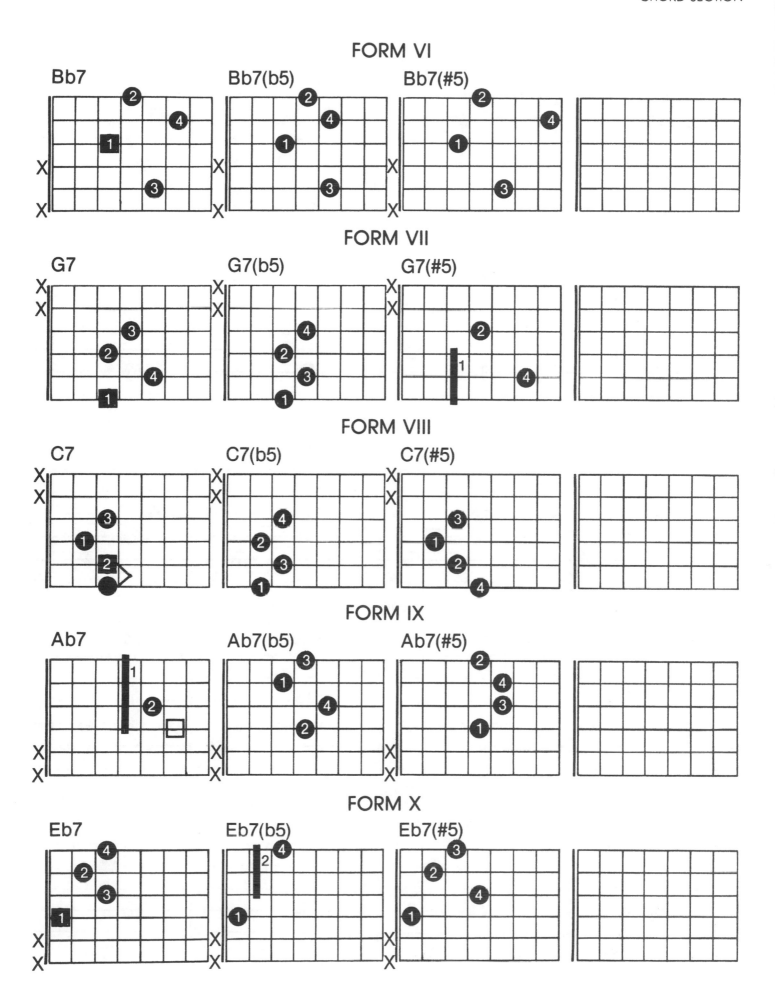

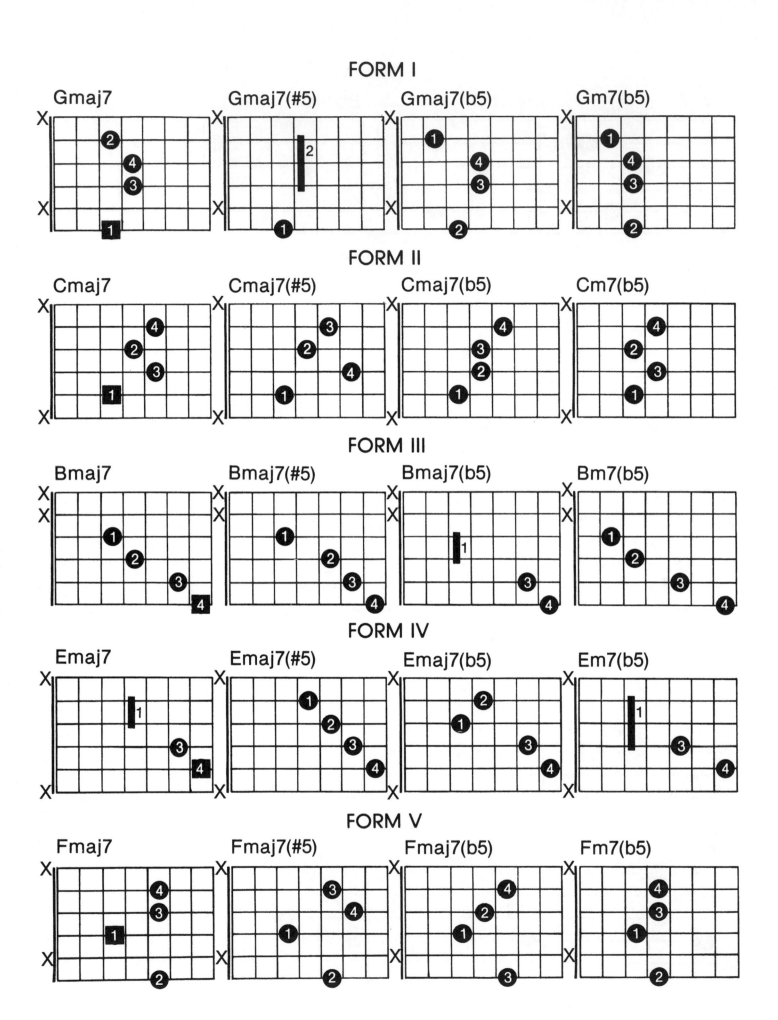

36

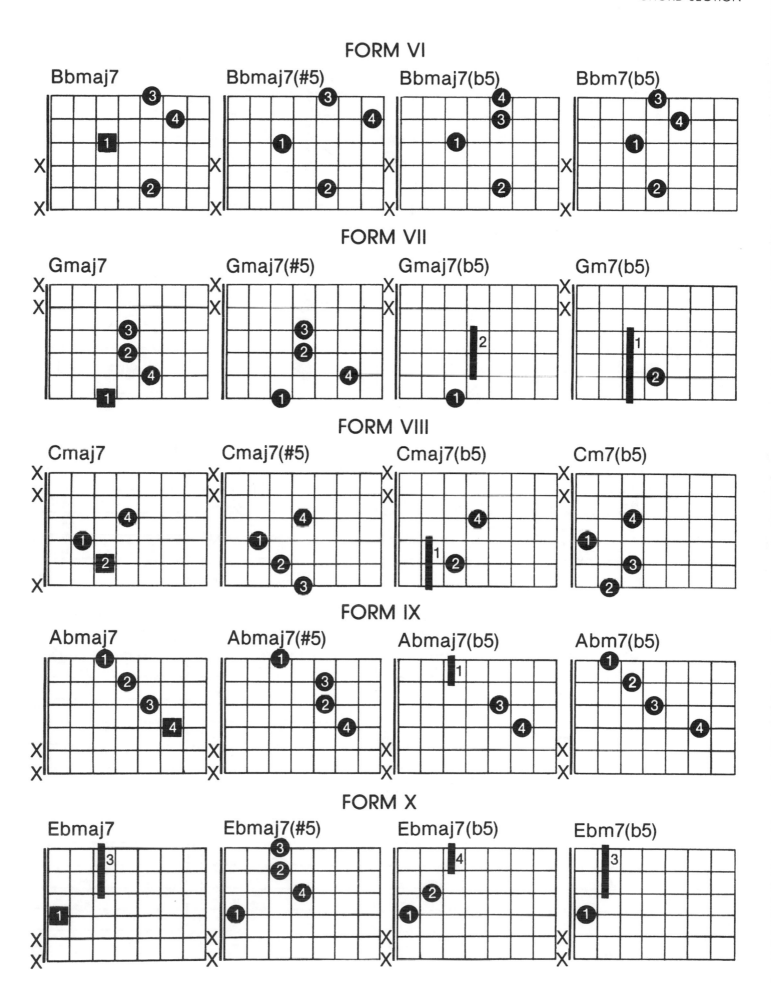

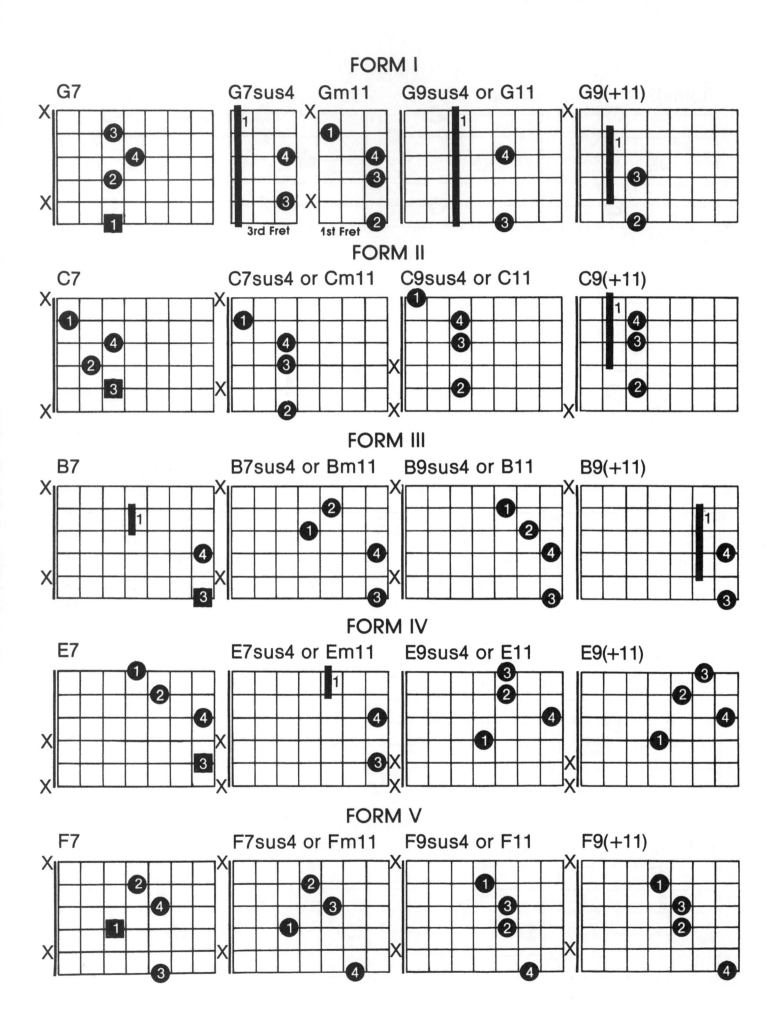

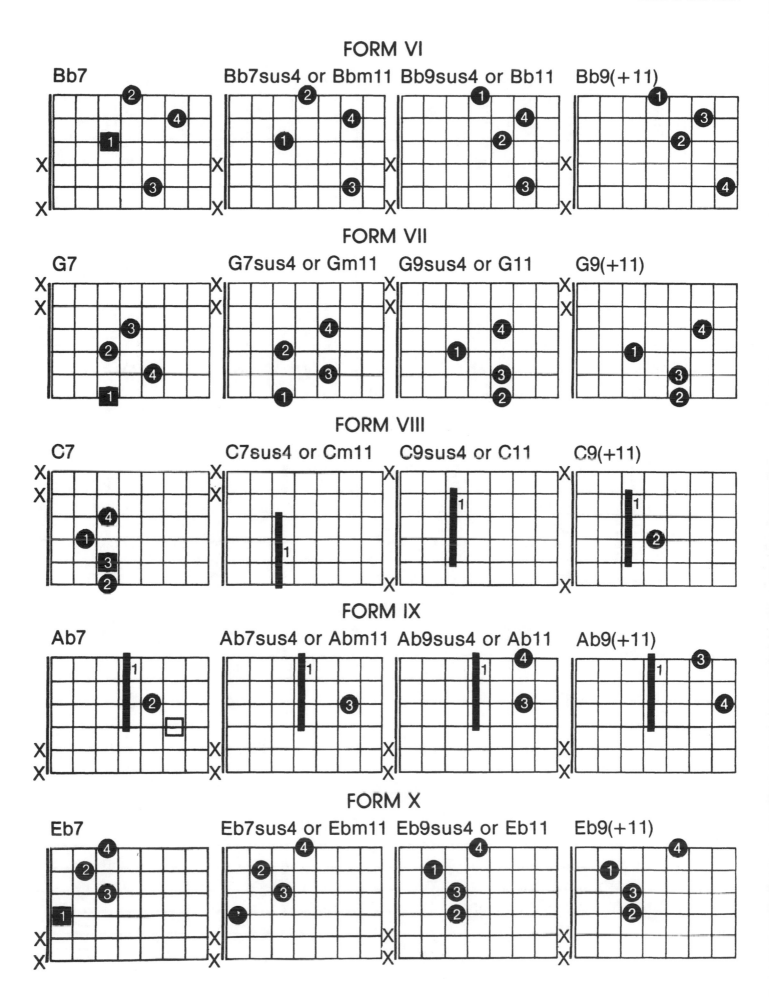

FORM VI

Bb7   Bb7sus4 or Bbm11   Bb9sus4 or Bb11   Bb9(+11)

FORM VII

G7   G7sus4 or Gm11   G9sus4 or G11   G9(+11)

FORM VIII

C7   C7sus4 or Cm11   C9sus4 or C11   C9(+11)

FORM IX

Ab7   Ab7sus4 or Abm11   Ab9sus4 or Ab11   Ab9(+11)

FORM X

Eb7   Eb7sus4 or Ebm11   Eb9sus4 or Eb11   Eb9(+11)

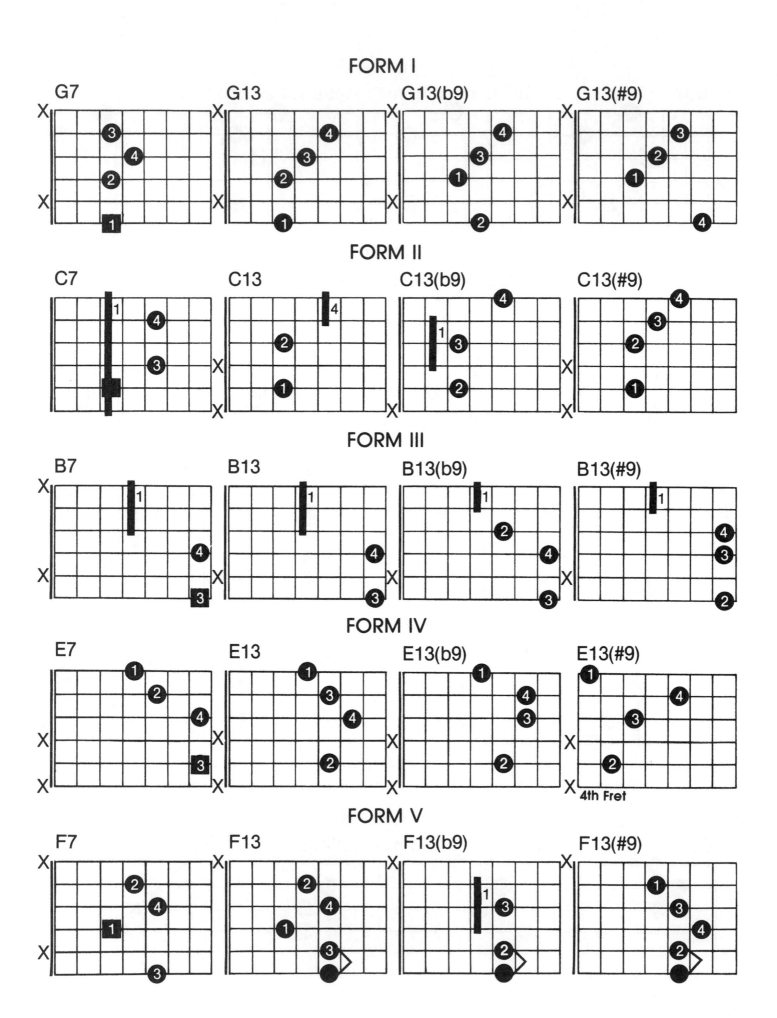

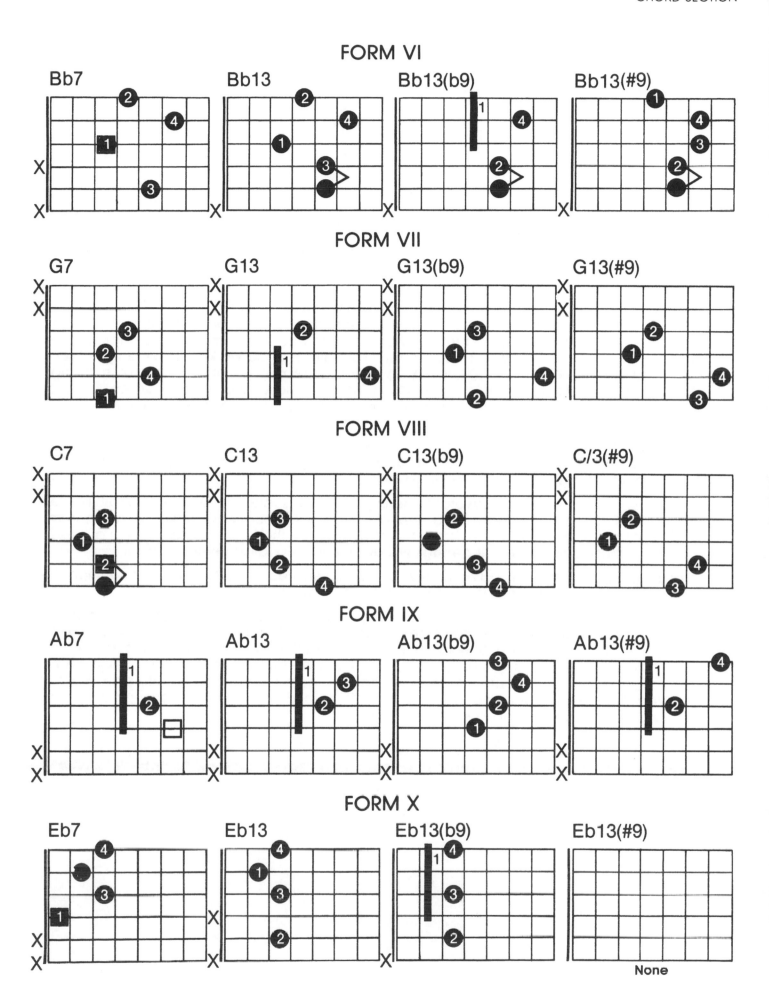

SCALE SECTION

As you look through this section, you will see many different scales or modes. In order to effectively solo over different chord progressions, first, as we mentioned before, having a good working knowledge of chords is definitely a **must** for good rhythm accompaniment, lead improvisation, and chord/melody, but second, a good soloist must have a good working knowledge of scales. Scales are used in developing leads, in linking melodic ideas together, and as fill-ins, linking chords and melodies together in chord/melody. The lead player should know which scale to play over a given chord or progression of chords. (This is discussed in the Master Guide to Chord/Scale Relationships on page 106.)

The first page of this section begins with the Major Scales with two basic Forms. Form I works in the Key of A Major, having a sixth string root and five fingerings, and Form II works in the Key of D Major, with a fifth string root and three fingerings.

The reason why we are showing several fingerings for each scale is to help you to familiarize yourself with the entire fingerboard and to enable you, as a good lead player, to move from one scale to another smoothly in any key and in any position on the fingerboard. Having a good knowledge of these **scales** and **fingerings** will **definitely** help to **achieve** this goal.

When practicing the different scales, unless it is absolutely necessary to change one finger for another, try to stay as close to our fingering patterns as possible.

Important Note: When practicing scales, take your time and **don't** just memorize the scales by the different patterns alone. **Read** the notes on the staff. Remember, practice each scale slowly, and get each note clear and clean. Speed will come in time. We suggest practicing scales in short intervals (approximately ten minutes) so you don't strain the muscles in your arm. Sitting and ripping through scales until your arms feel like they are going to fall off is an **old practicing theory** and a **bad one.** We use the same theory for practicing chords, scales, and arpeggios as they use in physical fitness programs, don't strain, but train.

Fingerboard

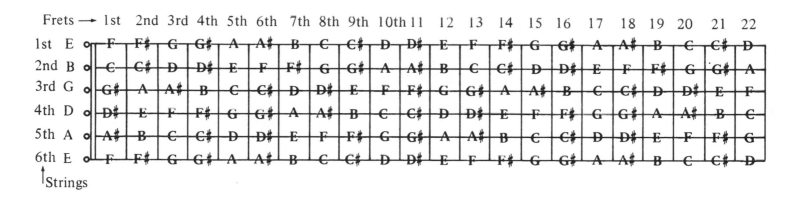

Frets →	1st	2nd	3rd	4th	5th	6th	7th	8th	9th	10th	11	12	13	14	15	16	17	18	19	20	21	22
1st E	F	F♯	G	G♯	A	A♯	B	C	C♯	D	D♯	E	F	F♯	G	G♯	A	A♯	B	C	C♯	D
2nd B	C	C♯	D	D♯	E	F	F♯	G	G♯	A	A♯	B	C	C♯	D	D♯	E	F	F♯	G	G♯	A
3rd G	G♯	A	A♯	B	C	C♯	D	D♯	E	F	F♯	G	G♯	A	A♯	B	C	C♯	D	D♯	E	F
4th D	D♯	E	F	F♯	G	G♯	A	A♯	B	C	C♯	D	D♯	E	F	F♯	G	G♯	A	A♯	B	C
5th A	A♯	B	C	C♯	D	D♯	E	F	F♯	G	G♯	A	A♯	B	C	C♯	D	D♯	E	F	F♯	G
6th E	F	F♯	G	G♯	A	A♯	B	C	C♯	D	D♯	E	F	F♯	G	G♯	A	A♯	B	C	C♯	D

↑Strings

Major Scales

Form I

A Major Scale (5) Fingerings (6)th String root

(A)

(B)

(C)

Major Scales

(D)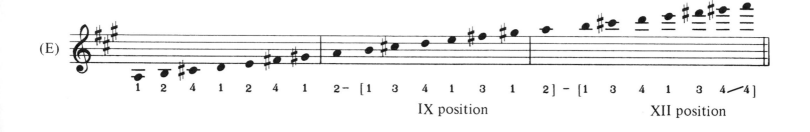

(E)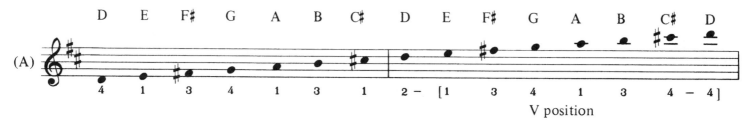

IX position   XII position

Form II
D Major Scale (3) Fingerings (5) String root

(A)

D	E	F♯	G	A	B	C♯	D	E	F♯	G	A	B	C♯	D

4 1 3 4 1 3 1 2 — [1 3 4 1 3 4 — 4]

V position

(B)

2 4 1 2 4 1 3 4 [1 3 4 1 3 4 — 4]

V position

(C)

1 2 4 1 2 4 1 — [1 3 1 2 4 1 3 4]

VII position

Note: All scale fingerings should be practiced ascending and descending in all keys and in eighth notes, eighth note triplets, broken thirds and sixteenth notes.

44

Major Scale Exercises A

A Major Scale 2 Octaves

2 Octave Scales

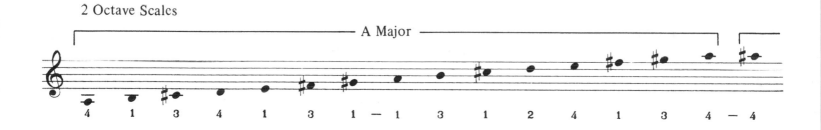

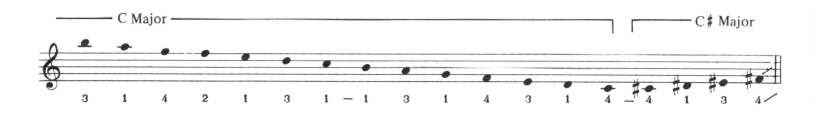

Major Scale Exercises B

Eighth Note Exercise

4 1 3 4 1 3 1 — 1 3 1 2 4 1 3 4

Eighth Note Triplet Exercise

3 *3* *3* *3* *3* *3* *3*

4 1 3 1 3 4 3 4 1 4 1 3 1 3 1 2 1 2 4

3 *3* *3* *3* *3* *3*

1 3 1 3 1 2 1 2 4 2 4 1 4 1 3 1 3 4

Note: All exercises use the form I-A fingering. Once this has been mastered, then work these exercises in all the other fingering.

Broken Thirds In Eighth Notes

4 3 1 4 3 1 4 3 2 1 4 2 1 4 1 1 3 2 1 4 2 1 4 3 1 4

Sixteenth Note Exercise

4 1 3 4 1 3 4 1 3 4 1 3 4 1 3 1 2 4 1 2 4 1 2 4

1 — 1 3 1 1 3 1 2 2 3 1 2 4 1 2 4 1 2 4 1 3 4 1 3 4 1 3 4 4 4

Pentatonic Scales

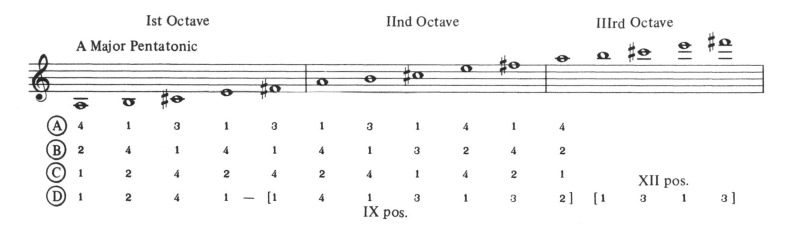

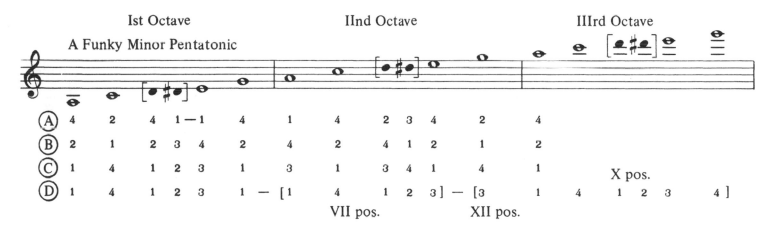

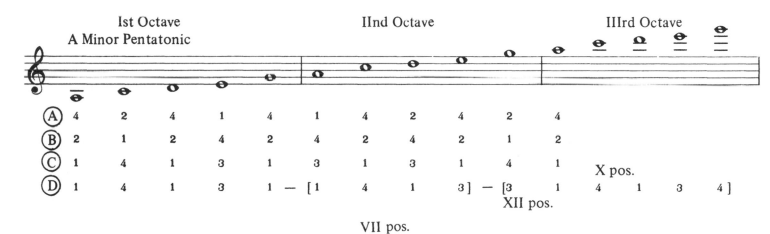

Working (6) Major Scales from (1) Position

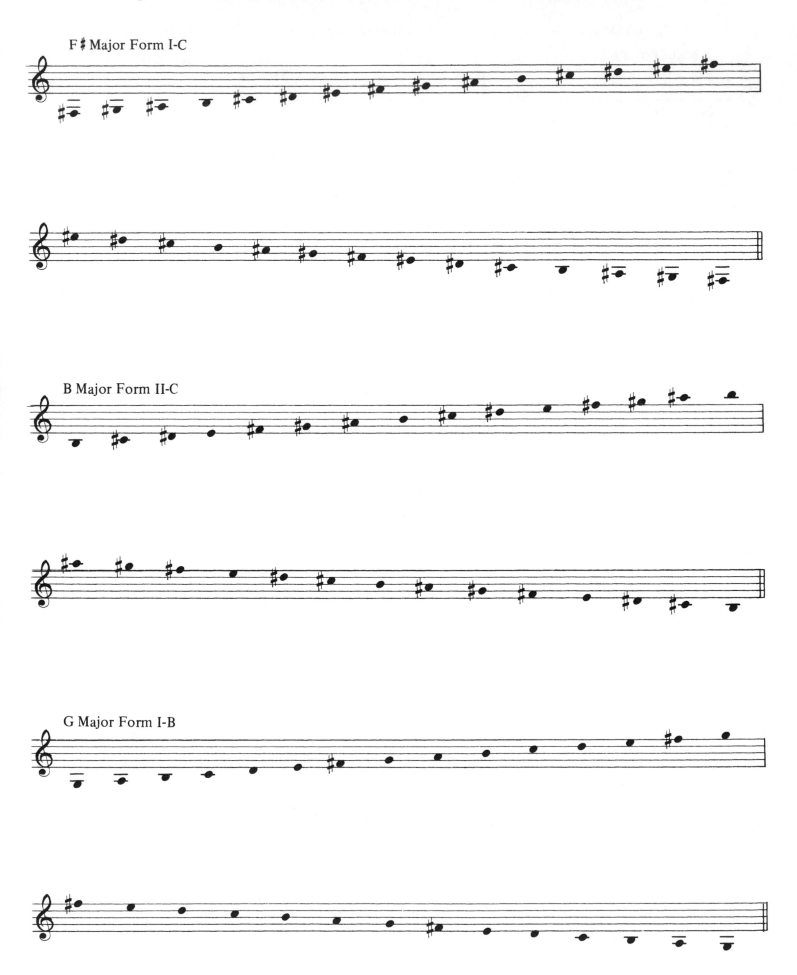

F♯ Major Form I-C

B Major Form II-C

G Major Form I-B

Working (6) Major Scales from (1) Position

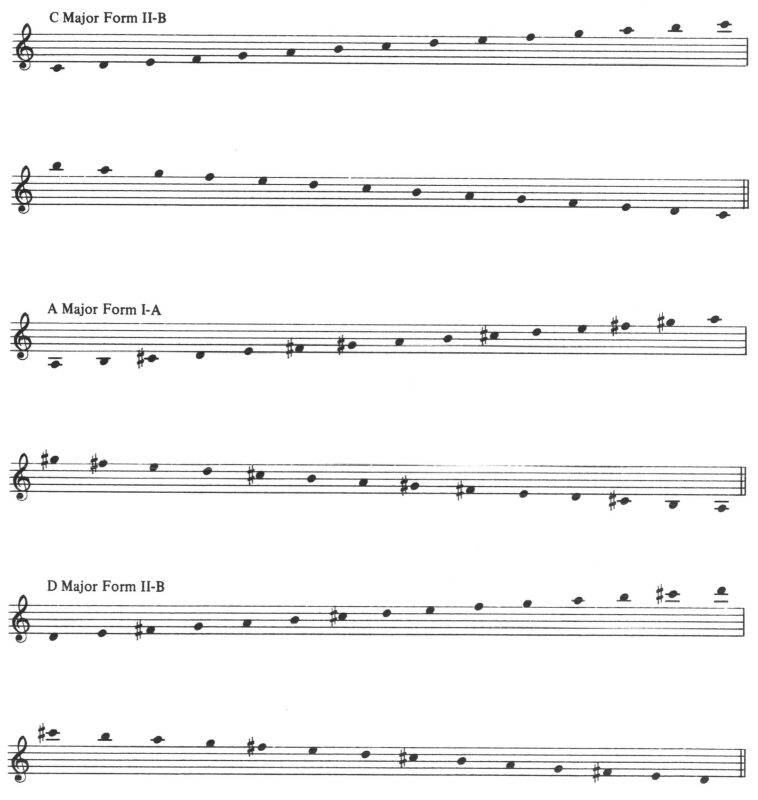

Note: The above exercise is worked from the IInd position. Remember: The 1st finger determines the position you're in, and not necessarily the root of the scale.

Note: Once the above exercise has been mastered and memorized, in the IInd pos., then repeat the entire exercise from the III, IV, V, VI, positions.

Modes With (6th) String Root

A Major Scale

A Ionian

B Dorian

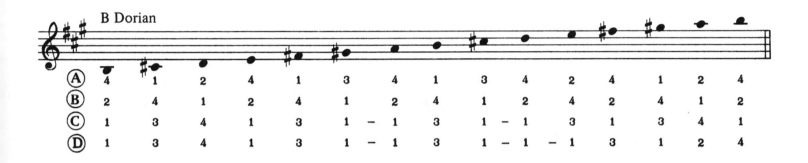

C♯ Phrygian

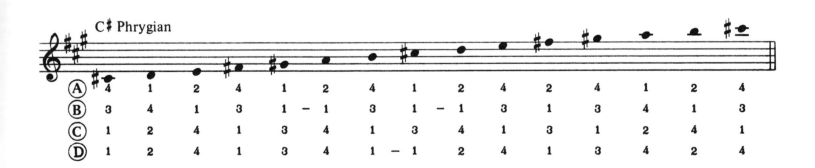

D Lydian

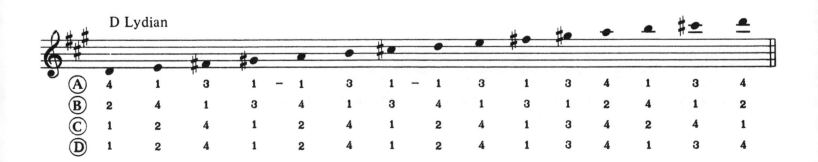

Modes With (6th) String Root

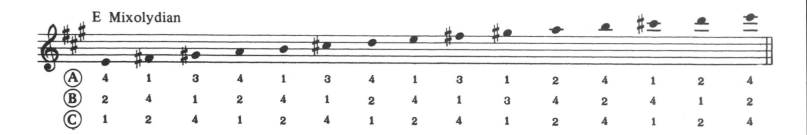

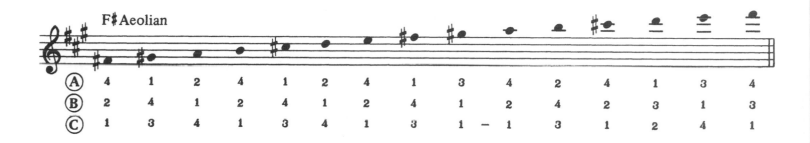

Modes

MODES — The word mode simply means scale. Modes are scales built from each individual note of a Major Scale. However, because these scales are built from one scale, they ALL share the same key signature.

EXAMPLE: D dorian is really a C Major Scale starting from D and ending on D an octave higher. Remember the D dorian mode differs from the D Major Scale which has two (2) sharps, F and C.

Pure Minor Scales

Form I Fingerings (6th) String Root

A minor (Pure)

(A)

4   1   2   4   1   2   4   1   3   4   2   4   1   2   4

(B)

2   4   1   2   4   1   3   4   1   2   4   2   2   1   2

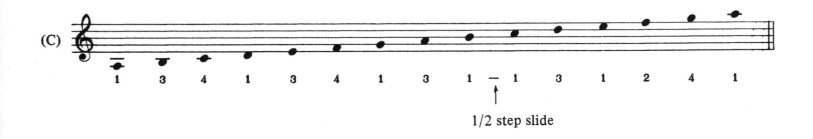

(C)

1   3   4   1   3   4   1   3   1 — 1   3   1   2   4   1

1/2 step slide

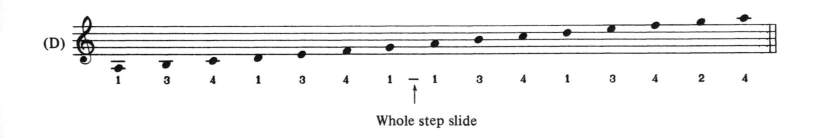

(D)

1   3   4   1   3   4   1 — 1   3   4   1   3   4   2   4

Whole step slide

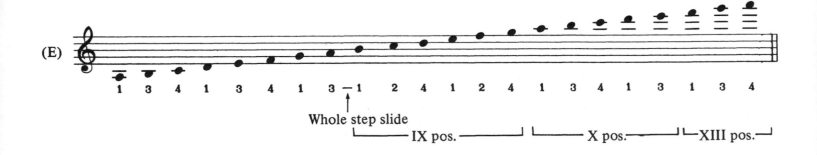

(E)

1   3   4   1   3   4   1   3 — 1   2   4   1   2   4   1   3   4   1   3   1   3   4

Whole step slide

└─── IX pos. ───┘ └─── X pos. ───┘ └─XIII pos.─┘

Pure Minor Scales

Form II Fingerings (5th) String Root

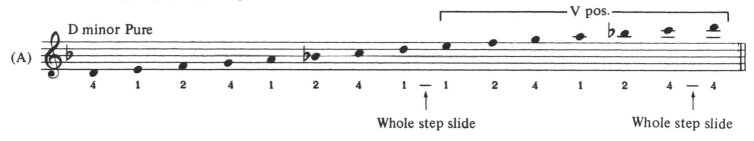

Harmonic Minor Scales

Form I Fingerings (6th) String Root
A minor (Harmonic)

(A)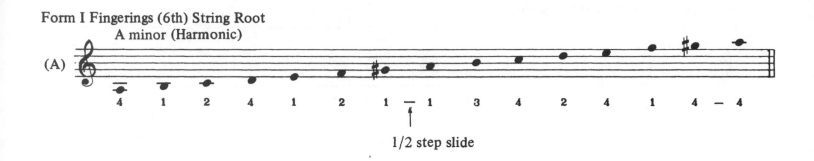

1/2 step slide

(B)

(C)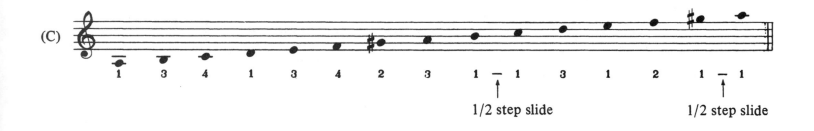

1/2 step slide   1/2 step slide

(D)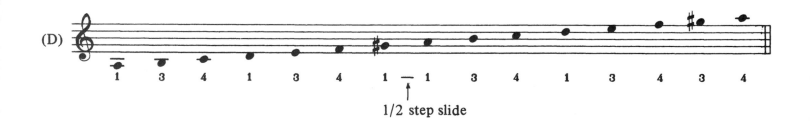

1/2 step slide

(E)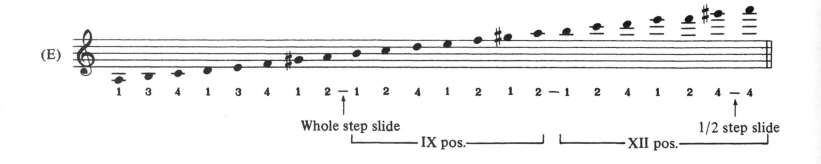

Whole step slide   1/2 step slide
└── IX pos. ──┘   └── XII pos. ──┘

Harmonic Minor Scales

Form II Fingerings (5th) String Root

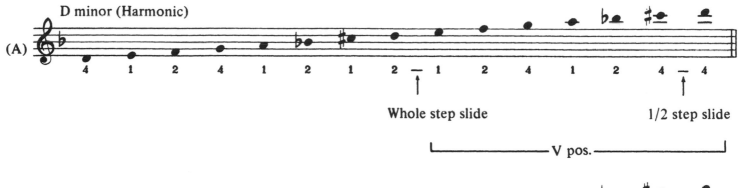

D minor (Harmonic)

(A)

4 1 2 4 1 2 1 2 — 1 2 4 1 2 4 — 4

Whole step slide   1/2 step slide

└─────── V pos. ───────┘

(B)

2 4 1 2 4 1 3 4 1 2 4 1 2 4 — 4

(C)

1 3 4 1 3 4 2 3 1 2 4 1 2 4 — 4

Jazz Melodic Minor Scales

Form I 6th String Root
    A minor

(A)

4   1   2   4   1   3   1   — 1   3   4   2   4   1   3   4

1/2 step slide

(B)

2   4   1   2   4   1   3   4   1   2   4   2   4   1   2

(C)

1   3   4   1   3   4   2   3   1   — 1   3   1   3   1   2

1/2 step slide

(D)

1   3   4   1   3   4   1   — 1   3   4   1   3   1   3   4

1/2 step slide

(E)

1   3   4   1   3   4   1   2 — 1   2   4   1   3   1   2 — 1   2   4   1   3   4 — 4

Whole step slide   1/2 step slide

Jazz Melodic Minor Scales

Form II 5th String Root

D minor

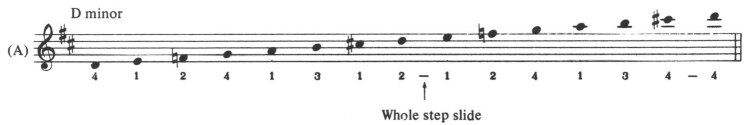

(A)

4   1   2   4   1   3   1   2   —   1   2   4   1   3   4   —   4

Whole step slide

(B)

2   4   1   2   4   1   3   4   1   2   4   1   3   4   —   4

1/2 step slide

(C)

1   3   4   1   3   4   1   —   1   3   4   2   4   1   3   4

1/2 step slide

Diminished Scales

Whole Step/Half Step

(A)

4   1   2   4   1   3   4   1 — 1   3   4   2   3   1 — 1   3   4

(B)

2   4   1   2   3   1 — 1   3   4   1   2   4   1   3   4   1   2

(C)

1   3   4   1   2   4   1   3   4   1   2   4   1   3   4   1   2

(D)

1   3   4   1 — 1   3   4   1 — 1   3   4   1 — 1   3   4   1 — 1   3   4   1 — 1   3   4 — 4 — 4

Diminished Scales

Half step/Whole step

(A)

(B)

(C)

(D)

Whole Tone Scales

(A)

4   1   3   1   3   4   1   3   1   3   1   3   4

3   1   3   1   3   1   4   2   1   3   1   4

(B)

2   4   1   3   1   2   4   1   3   1   3   1   3

1   3   1   3   1   4   2   1   3   1   4   2

(C)

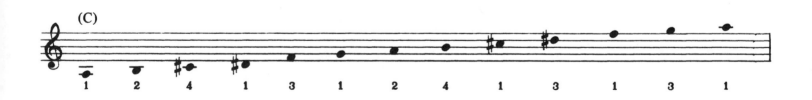

1   2   4   1   3   1   2   4   1   3   1   3   1

3   1   3   1   4   2   1   3   1   4   2   1

Whole Tone Scales

Note: Work these fingerings in eighth notes, eighth note triplets, broken thirds, and sixteenth notes.

Remember! Any note in a whole tone scale may be considered the root.

ARPEGGIO SECTION

We would like to begin this section by giving a simple definition of an Arpeggio. An arpeggio is built from the tones that make up a chord but are picked as individual notes. They may be used as leads and as fill-ins, linking melodies with chords in chord/melody.

Just like scales, all the fingering patterns **must** be practiced and memorized in every position and in every key. Again, unless it is absolutely necessary to change a finger or two, stay with our fingering patterns, and **don't** just memorize the fingerings. Read the notes on the staff. The use of arpeggios will be discussed in the Master Guide to Chord/Arpeggio Relationships on page 108.

Form I Arpeggio Studies (6th) String Root

A Major

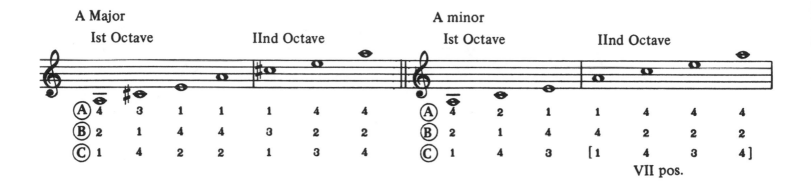

A minor

A Major 7

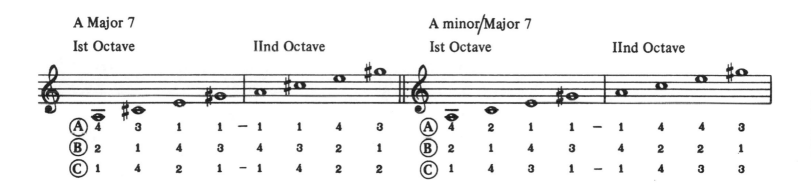

A minor/Major 7

A7

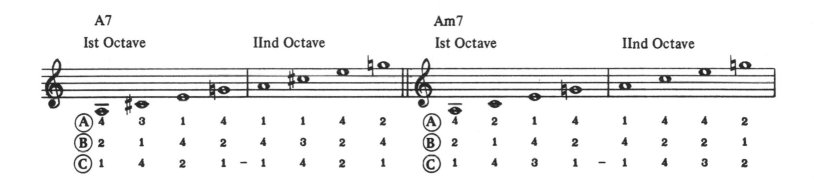

Am7

Form I Arpeggio Studies (6th) String Root

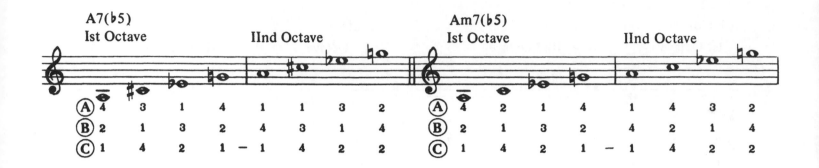

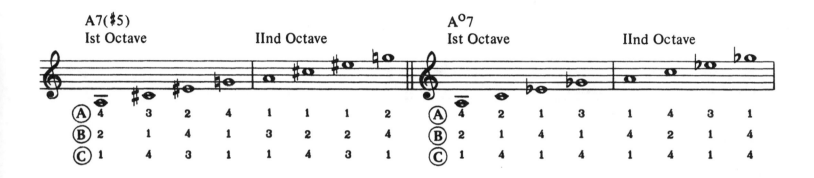

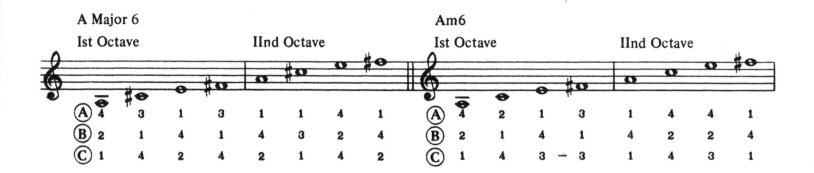

Form I Arpeggio Studies 1

Ex I (A)

Ex I (B)

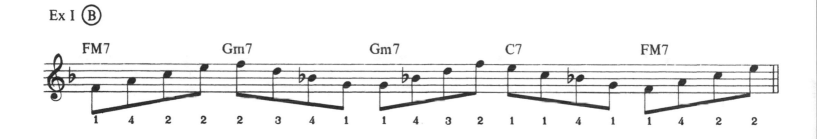

Ex I (C)

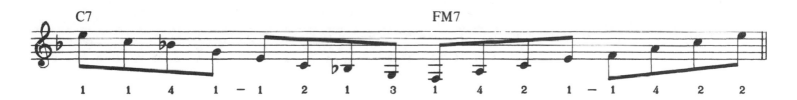

Note: Each exercise should be memorized in every key.

Form I Arpeggio Studies 2

Ex 2 - Ⓐ

Ex 2 - Ⓑ

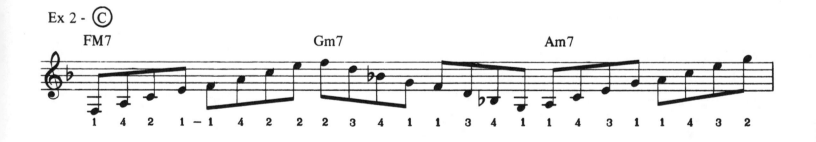

Ex 2 - Ⓒ

Form I Arpeggio Studies 3

Ex 3 - Ⓐ

Ex 3 - Ⓑ

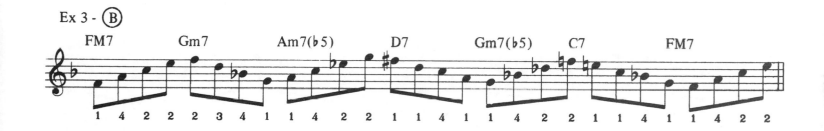

Ex 3 - Ⓒ

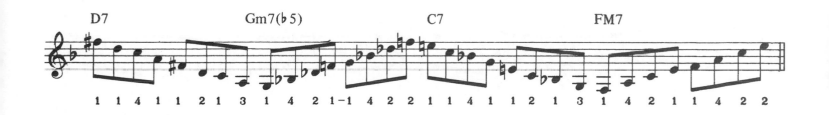

Form I Arpeggio Studies 4

Ex 4 - Ⓐ

Ex 4 - Ⓑ

Ex 4 - Ⓒ

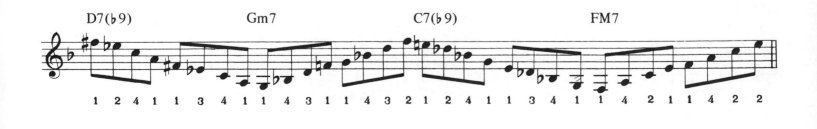

Form I Arpeggio Studies 5, 6 & 7

Ex. 5

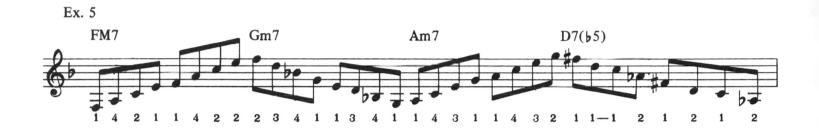

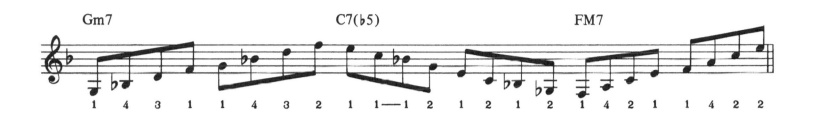

Ex. 6

Ex. 7

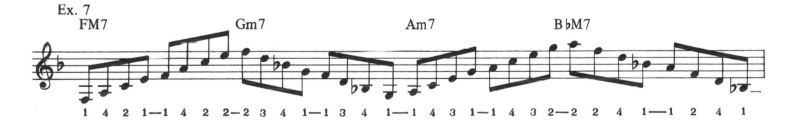

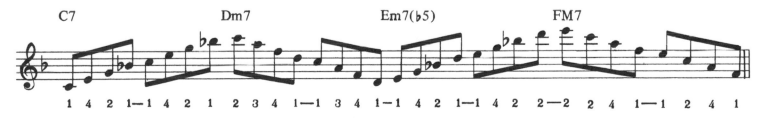

Form II Arpeggio Studies (5th) String Root

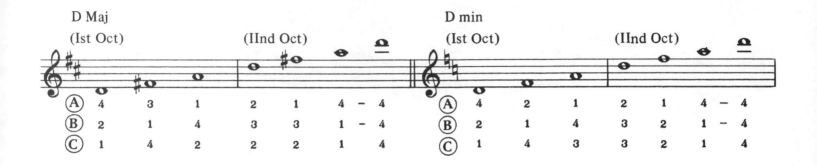

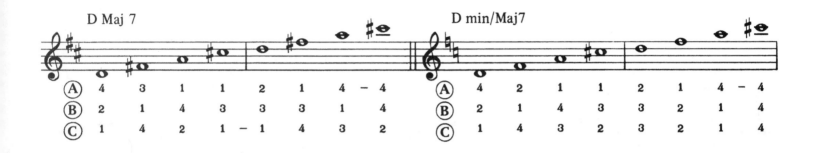

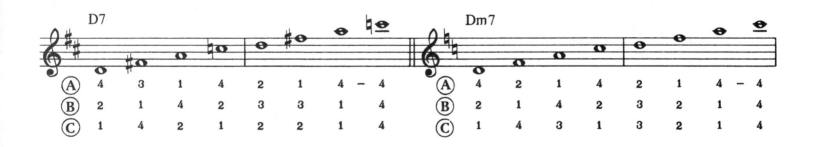

Form II Arpeggio Studies (5th) String Root

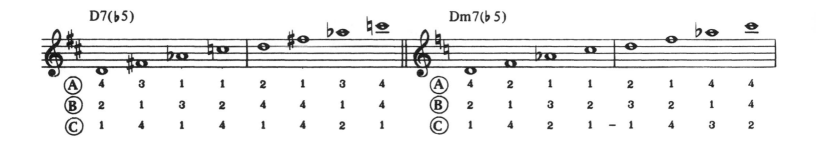

D7(♭5)

Ⓐ	4	3	1	1	2	1	3	4
Ⓑ	2	1	3	2	4	4	1	4
Ⓒ	1	4	1	4	1	4	2	1

Dm7(♭5)

Ⓐ	4	2	1	1	2	1	4	4
Ⓑ	2	1	3	2	3	2	1	4
Ⓒ	1	4	2	1	–	1	4	3	2

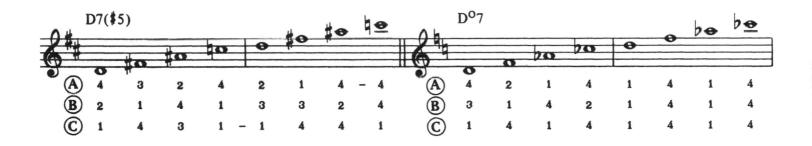

D7(♯5)

Ⓐ	4	3	2	4	2	1	4	–	4
Ⓑ	2	1	4	1	3	3	2	4
Ⓒ	1	4	3	1	–	1	4	4	1

Dᵒ7

Ⓐ	4	2	1	4	1	4	1	4
Ⓑ	3	1	4	2	1	4	1	4
Ⓒ	1	4	1	4	1	4	1	4

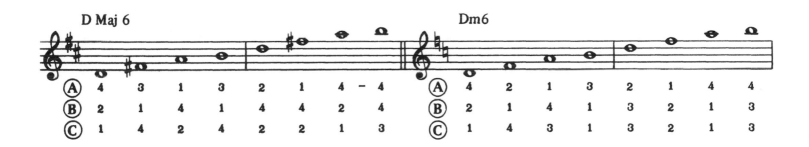

D Maj 6

Ⓐ	4	3	1	3	2	1	4	–	4
Ⓑ	2	1	4	1	4	4	2	4
Ⓒ	1	4	2	4	2	2	1	3

Dm6

Ⓐ	4	2	1	3	2	1	4	4
Ⓑ	2	1	4	1	3	2	1	3
Ⓒ	1	4	3	1	3	2	1	3

Form II Arpeggio Studies 1

Ex I - Ⓐ

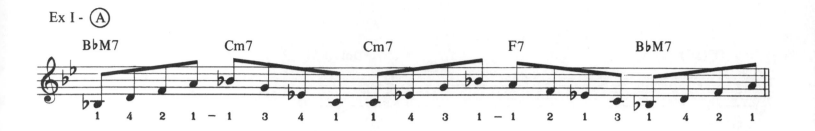

Ex I - Ⓑ

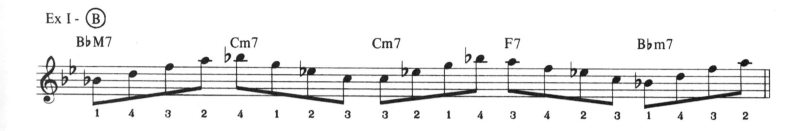

Ex 1 - Ⓒ

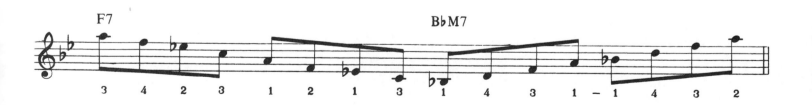

Form II Arpeggio Studies 2

Ex 2 - Ⓐ

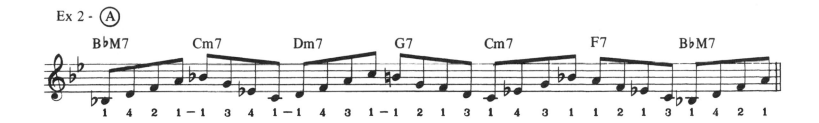

Ex 2 - Ⓑ

Ex 2 - Ⓒ

Form II Arpeggio Studies 3

Ex. - 3 - Ⓐ

Ex. - 3 - Ⓑ

Ex. - 3 - Ⓒ

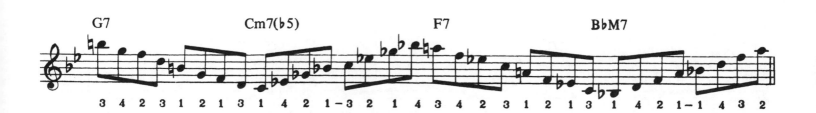

Form II Arpeggio Studies 4

Ex - 4 - Ⓐ

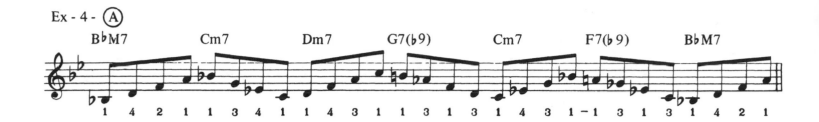

Ex - 4 - Ⓑ

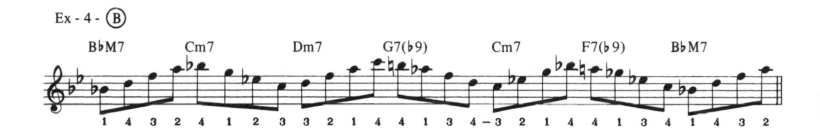

Ex - 4 - Ⓒ

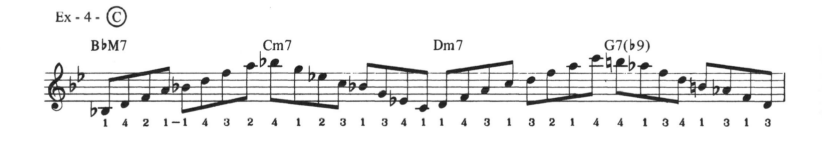

Form II Arpeggio Studies 5

Ex - 5 - Ⓐ

Ex - 5 - Ⓑ

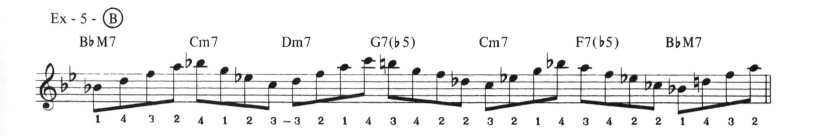

Ex - 5 - Ⓒ

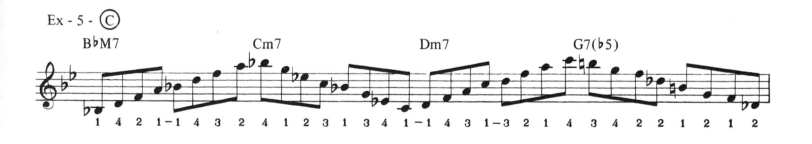

Form II Arpeggio Studies 6

Ex - 6 - Ⓐ

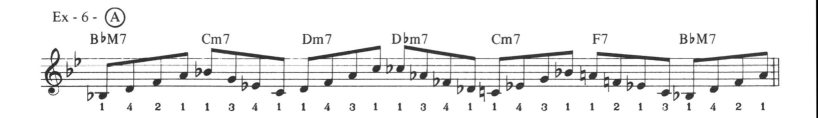

Ex - 6 - Ⓑ

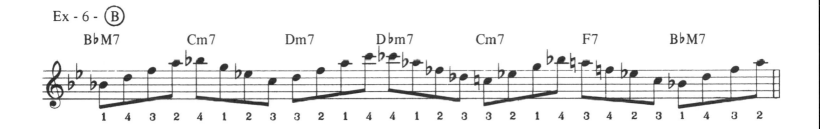

Ex - 6 - Ⓒ

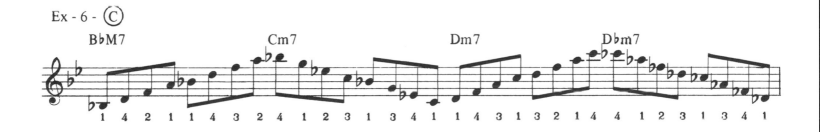

Form II Arpeggio Studies 7

Ex - 7 - Ⓐ

Ex - 7 - Ⓑ

Ex - 7 - Ⓒ

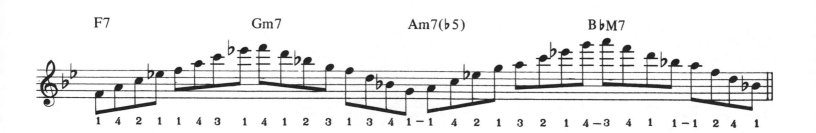

Jazz Chord Exercises One

Ex. - I
Form I

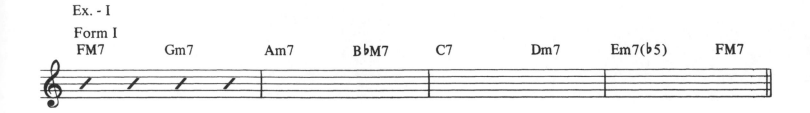

Ex. - II
Form II
II - A

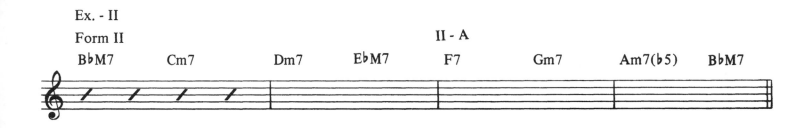

Ex.- III
Form I

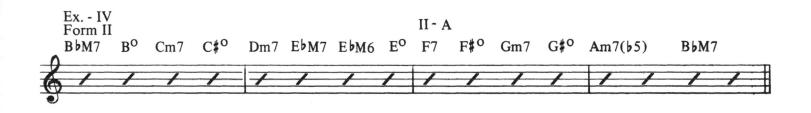

Ex. - IV
Form II
II - A

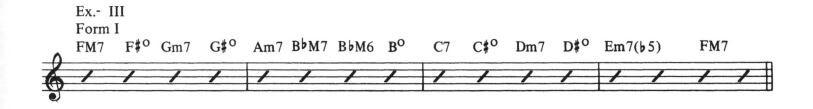

Ex. - V

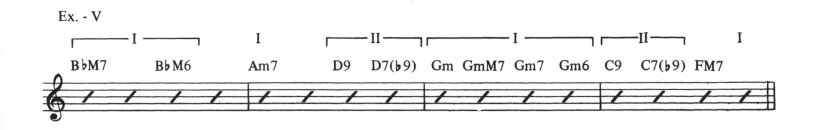

Jazz Chord Exercises One

Ex. - VI

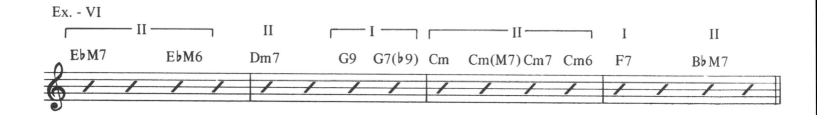

Ex. -VII

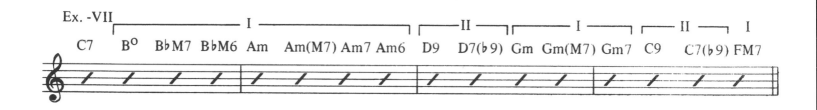

Ex. - VIII

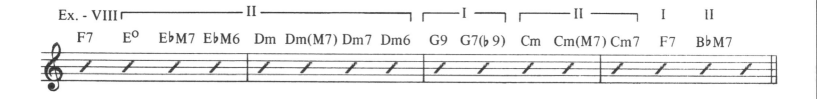

Ex. - IX

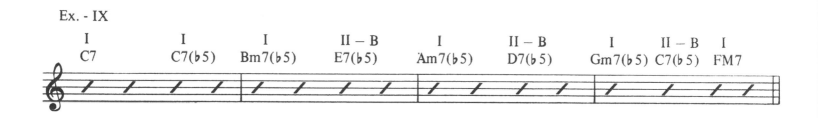

Ex. - X

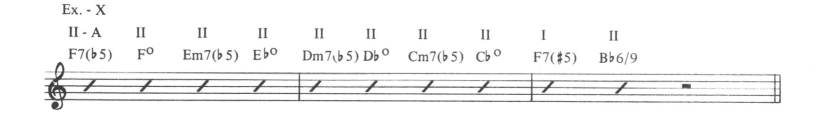

Jazz Chord Exercises Two

Ex. - I
Form III

AM7   Bm7   C#m7   DM7   E7   F#m7   G#m(♭5)   AM7

Ex. - II
Form III

E7   DM7   DM6   C#m7   C#m6   Bm7   Bm6   AM7   AM6

Ex. - III
Form IV

DM7   Em7   F#m7   GM7   A7   Bm7   C#m7(♭5)   DM7

Ex. - IV
Form IV

A7   GM7   GM6   F#m7   F#m6   Em7   Em6   DM7   DM6

Ex. - V
Form V

E♭M7   Fm7   Gm7   A♭M7   B♭7   Cm7   Dm7(♭5)   E♭M7

Ex. - VI
Form V

B♭7   A♭M7   A♭M6   Gm7   Gm6   Fm7   Fm6   E♭M7   E♭M6

Jazz Chord Exercises Two

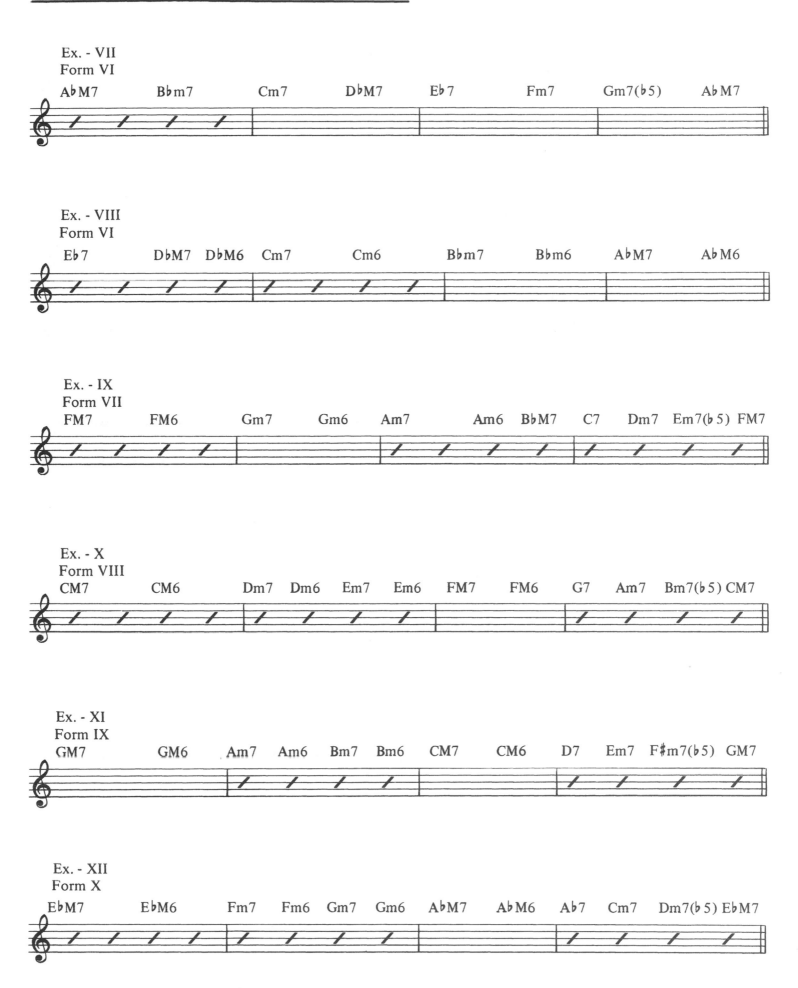

Ex. - VII
Form VI

| A♭M7 | B♭m7 | Cm7 | D♭M7 | E♭7 | Fm7 | Gm7(♭5) | A♭M7 |

Ex. - VIII
Form VI

| E♭7 | D♭M7 D♭M6 | Cm7 | Cm6 | B♭m7 | B♭m6 | A♭M7 | A♭M6 |

Ex. - IX
Form VII

| FM7 | FM6 | Gm7 | Gm6 | Am7 | Am6 B♭M7 | C7 | Dm7 Em7(♭5) FM7 |

Ex. - X
Form VIII

| CM7 | CM6 | Dm7 Dm6 | Em7 Em6 | FM7 | FM6 | G7 | Am7 | Bm7(♭5) CM7 |

Ex. - XI
Form IX

| GM7 | GM6 | Am7 Am6 | Bm7 Bm6 | CM7 | CM6 | D7 | Em7 F♯m7(♭5) GM7 |

Ex. - XII
Form X

| E♭M7 | E♭M6 | Fm7 Fm6 | Gm7 Gm6 | A♭M7 | A♭M6 | A♭7 | Cm7 | Dm7(♭5) E♭M7 |

12 BAR BLUES &
AL DI MEOLA TUNES

We feel that this section of the System is not only the most interesting and rewarding one, but probably the section you'll enjoy and have the most fun studying. It is in this section that we give you the chance to learn how, when, and where to use the tools of your trade (chords, scales, and arpeggios). We will work with several interesting 12 Bar Blues patterns and some popular tunes written and recorded by Al. We felt that working with this material would be more fun to practice plus give you more of a practical working knowledge than a bunch of boring exercises.

The 12 Bar Blues patterns have two parts, A and B. The A part shows the basic chords to these blues progressions, and the B part gives you the chord substitutions and progressions. It is very important not only to memorize the chord substitutions and progressions in every position, but be able to eventually improvise over these changes.

Each tune has two parts, A and B. Part A lists the basic chord changes. Part B gives you the melody. These parts should be studied and practiced separately. The Roman numerals above each chord represent the chord forms we feel make the fullest sounding rhythm chords and create the best flowing cycle progression. However, once you've mastered the chord forms we've provided, we strongly suggest going through each tune and experimenting with other forms.

Remember, once parts A and B have been memorized in each tune, then begin to improvise over the basic chord changes using the scales and arpeggios you've studied. The chord changes of a tune must be memorized in order to really improvise effectively.

A Practice Tip: We suggest using two cassette decks when practicing these tunes. First, record the rhythm accompaniment to the tune, then as the cassette plays back the rhythm chords, use the second recorder to record yourself playing the melody against the chord changes. When you play back that tape, you'll get a better idea of how your timing is and just how well the melody is flowing. You can use this same practicing technique when working on your improvisation. While playing back the second tape deck or the finished product, you'll hear how you're matching the scales or arpeggios over the chords. This is an excellent aid in phrasing and correcting mistakes.

12 Bar Blues

Ex. -I

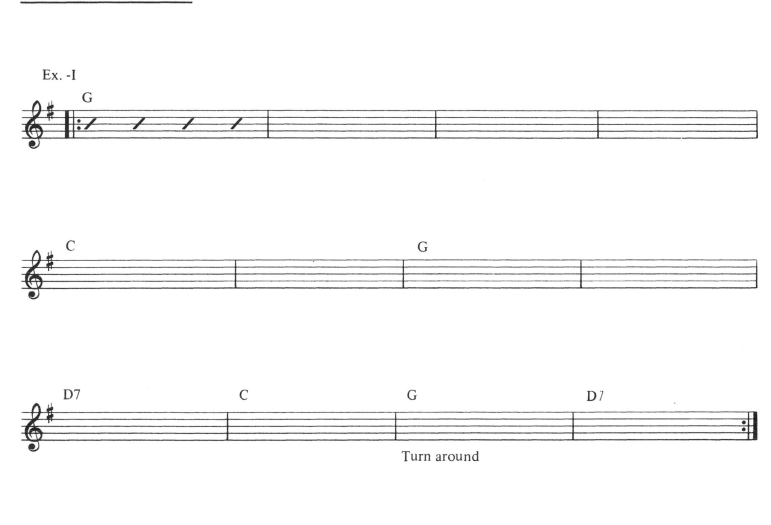

Turn around

Ex. - II

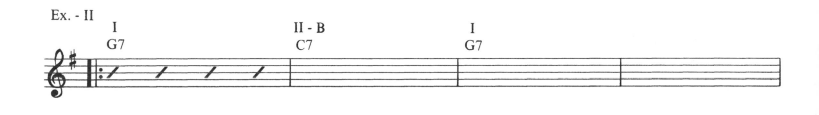

12 Bar Blues

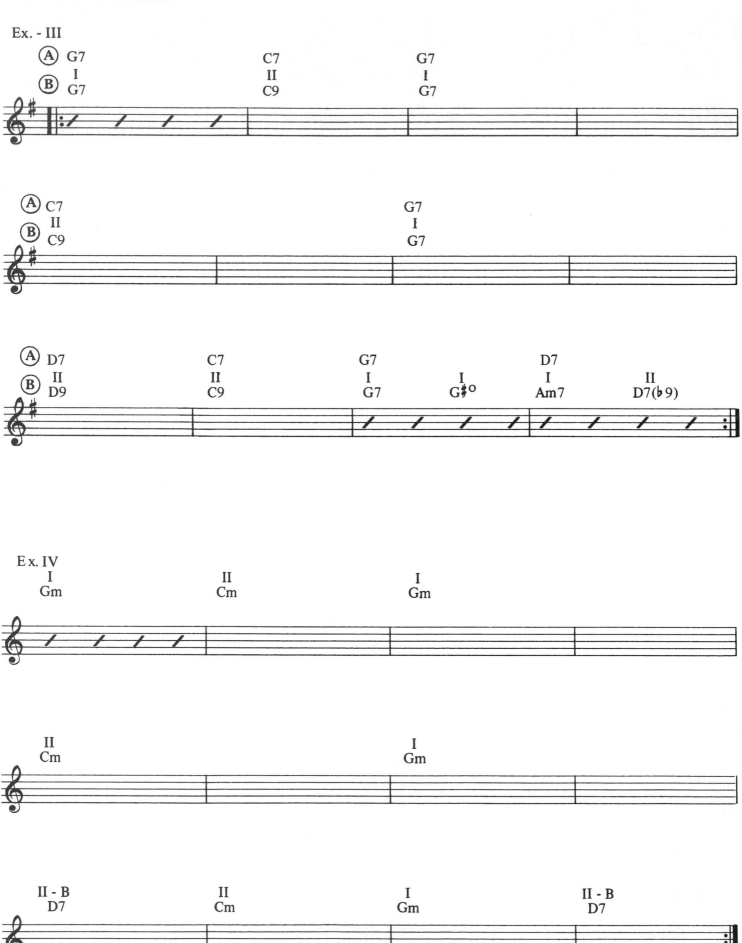

12 Bar Blues

Ex. V

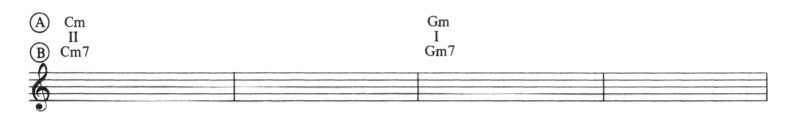

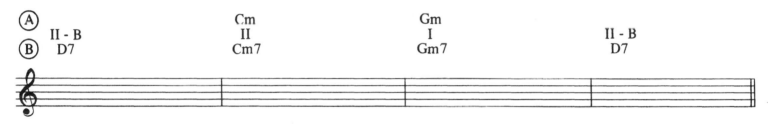

Ex. VI

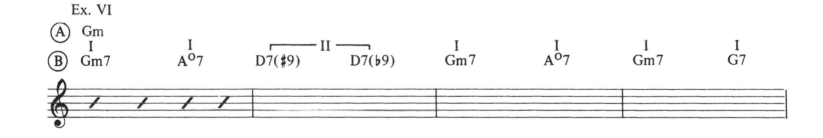

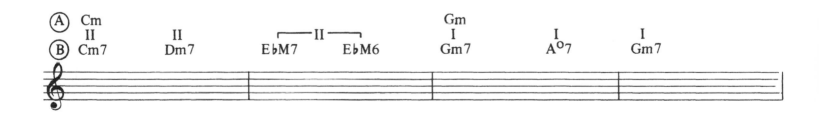

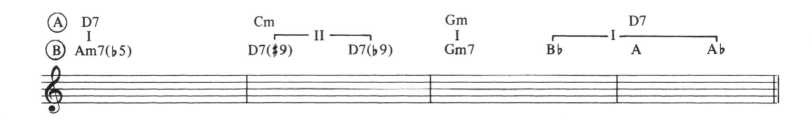

12 Bar Blues

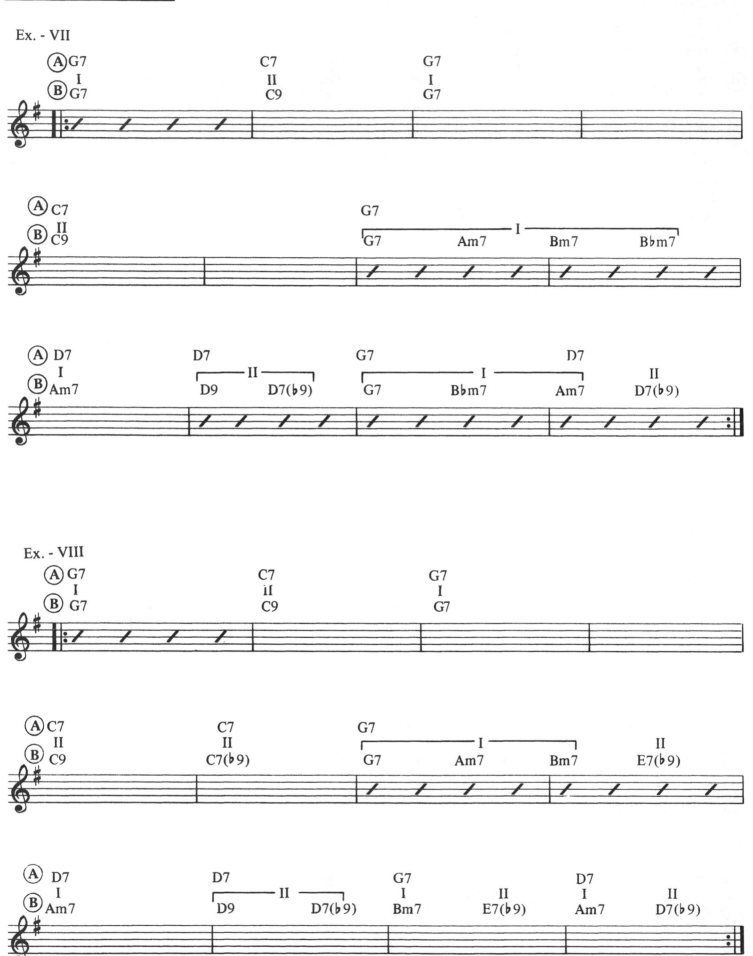

12 Bar Blues

12 Bar Blues

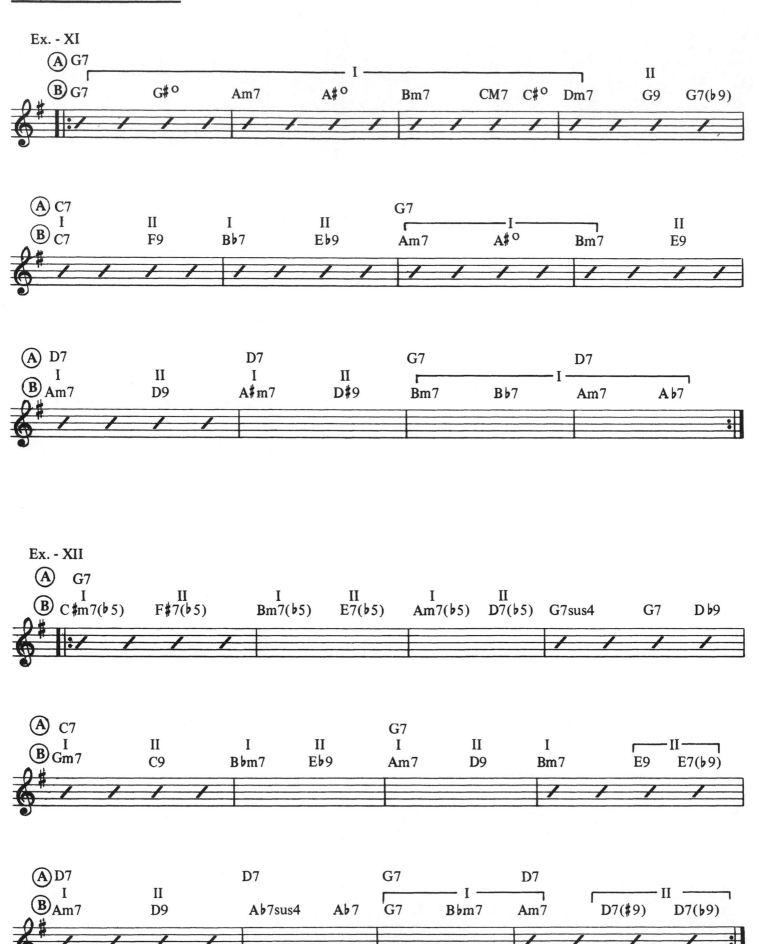

12 Bar Blues

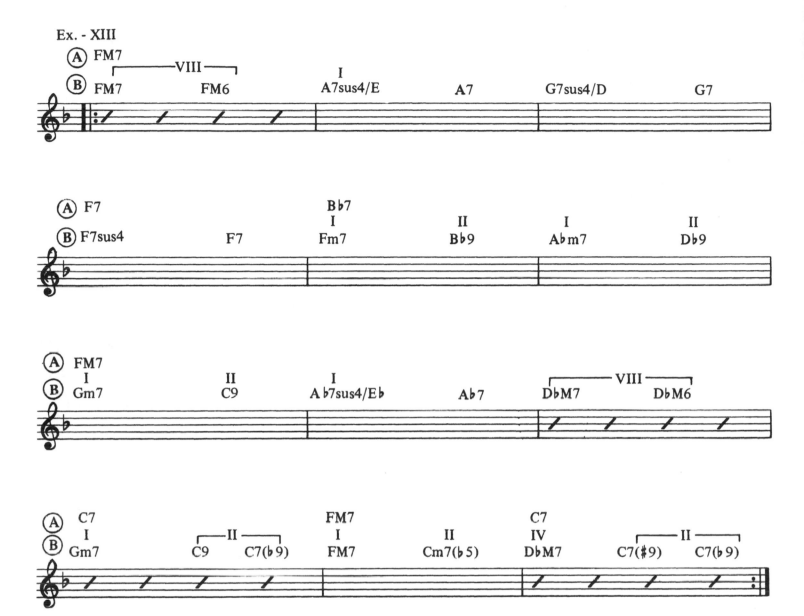

Ritmo De La Noche

Dinner Music of The Gods

* Optional background riff for guitar. Al's solos for M9-15, 18-24, and 27-32 are not given here. Please refer to the recording for Al's solos in these measures.

*Bass plays freely in a 12/8 mode, i.e.:

98

Note: F#sus4 = Fmaj Form I with sus4 - B♭ added.
Bsus4 = Bmaj Form I with sus4 - E added.

Al Di's Dream Theme

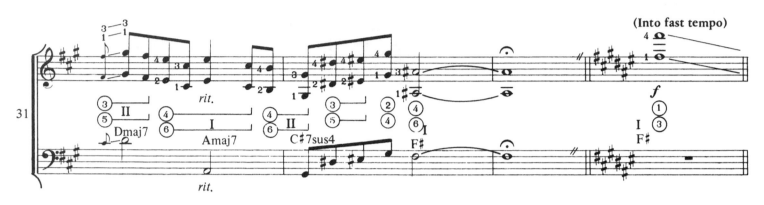

Lady Of Rome, Sister Of Brazil

MASTER GUIDE TO CHORD/SCALE RELATIONSHIPS

Before listing the different chord/scale relationships, we would like to mention a couple of simple things to remember when improvising. First, using the Key of C Major as an example, examine the notes of a C Major diatonic scale. Then turn back to your theory book and see how the chords in the Key of C Major are built from the C scale. These chords written in four part harmony would be CM7, Dm7, Em7, FM7, G7, Am7, Bm7(b5). Since these chords are all built from the notes of a C Major Scale, it is only logical that the C Major Scale would sound good played over all of these chords. So take your cassette player and record a simple progression in the Key of C such as CM7, Dm7, Em7, FM7, Em7, Dm7, G7, CM7, four strums each. Then try playing any form of the C Major Scale and see how it sounds. You'll be very surprised.

The second thing we would like to mention is the Chromatic Scale, which is a twelve note scale made up of ½ steps. It would seem obvious that since this scale covers every possible note in music, if you start from C low octave and go to high C two octaves higher, this scale would sound good over all the chords in the Key of C Major. There are no bad notes. Overplaying this scale does become boring and tastless though, so be careful how you use it.

Chord/Scale Relationships

Maj, Maj7, Maj6, Maj9

1) Pure Major Scale
2) Ionian Mode

Maj6/9

1) Major Pentatonic

Pure Minor as (I Tonic)

1) Aeolian Mode
2) Funky Minor Pentatonic
3) Minor Pentatonic
4) Phrygian Mode

Minor 7th (II Supertonic)

1) Dorian Mode
2) Minor Pentatonic
3) Funky Minor Pentatonic
4) Chromatic Minor Pentatonic
5) Whole Step - Half Step Diminished

Minor 7th (III Mediant)

1) Aeolian Mode
2) Phrygian Mode

Minor 7sus4

1) Dorian Mode
2) Funky Minor Pentatonic

Dom7 Unaltered

1) Mixolydian Mode
2) Major Pentatonic from Whole Step below Root
3) Minor Pentatonic from Root
4) Lydian Mode with flat 7th

Dom7(b5) - Dom7(#5)

1) Whole Tone Scale

Dom7sus4

1) Mixolydian Mode

Dom7(b9)

1) Half Step - Whole Step Diminished

Dom7(#9)

1) Half Step - Whole Step Diminished
2) Dorian Mode
3) Minor Pentatonic
4) Funky Minor Pentatonic

Minor/Maj7

1) Harmonic Minor Scale
2) Jazz Melodic Minor Scale

Minor 7(b5)

1) Locrian Mode
2) Whole Step - Half Step Diminished

Minor 6 and Minor 6/9

1) Jazz Melodic Minor
2) Minor Pentatonic
3) Funky Minor Pentatonic

Dim7

1) Whole Step - Half Step Diminished
2) Locrian

Dom9

1) Mixolydian Mode
2) Jazz Melodic Minor Scale
3) Minor Pentatonic from the 5th of chord
4) Funky Minor Pentatonic from the 5th of chord
5) Locrian Mode from the 3rd of chord

Dom9(+11)

1) Whole Tone Scale

Dom11

1) Mixolydian Mode

Minor 11

1) Aeolian Mode
2) Minor Pentatonic
3) Ionian Mode from the minor 3rd of chord

Dom 13

1) Mixolydian Mode
2) Jazz Melodic Minor Scale

Dom13(b9) or Dom13(#9)

1) Half Step - Whole Step Scale

MASTER GUIDE TO CHORD/ARPEGGIO RELATIONSHIPS

1) Pure Major Chord - _____Pure Major Arpeggio
2) Major 7th Chord - _____Major 7 Arpeggio
3) Major 6th Chord - _____Major 6 Arpeggio
4) Pure Minor Chord - _____Pure Minor Arpeggio
5) Minor/Major 7th Chord -____Minor/Major 7 Arpeggio
6) Minor 7th Chord - _____Minor 7 Arpeggio
7) Dom 7 Chord - _____Dom7 Arpeggio
8) Dom7(#5) Chord - _____Dom7(#5) Arpeggio
9) Dom7(b5) Chord - _____Dom7(b5) Arpeggio
10) Minor7(b5) Chord - _____Minor7(b5) Arpeggio
11) Dim7 Chord - _____Dim7 Arpeggio
12) Major 9th Chord - _____Minor 7 Arpeggio from 3rd of chord
13) Dom9 Chord - _____Minor 6 Arpeggio from 5th of chord
    Minor 7(b5) Arpeggio from 3rd of Chord
14) Dom7(b9) Chord - _____Diminished Arpeggio
15) Dom7(#9) Chord - _____Diminished Arpeggio

MASTER GUIDE TO CHORD SUBSTITUTIONS

Major Chords

Maj7, Maj6, Maj9 may be used carefully, and Maj6/9

Dorn7 Chords

Dom9, Dom11, Dom13

Dom9 Chords

Dom7, Dom11, Dom13

Minor Chords

Minor 7, Minor 6, Minor 9 used carefully
Minor, Minor/Major 7, Minor 7, Minor 6 progression

Chord Symbols

As you pick up different music books and sheet music, you will see the same chord names abbreviated different ways. It is our intention to list all the different chord name abbreviations. We will use the chord name G for all the examples below:

1) **G Major** — G; GM, GMaj
2) **G Major 7** — GM7; GMaj7; G7; GMajor7
3) **G Minor** — Gm; Gmin; G minor
4) **G Minor 7** — Gm7; Gmin7; G-7; Gminor7
5) **G Dominant 7** — G7; Gdom7
6) **G Major 6** — G6; GM6; GMaj6; GMajor6
7) **G Minor/Major 7** — GmM7; Gm7; GminM7; GmMaj7; Gmin/Maj7
8) **G Minor 7(b5)** — Gm7(b5); Gmin7(b5); G-7(b5); Gm7(−5)
9) **G Dominant 7(b5)** — G7(b5); Gdom(b5); G7(−5)
10) **G Dominant 7(#5)** — G7(#5); Gdom7(#5); G7(+5); Gdom(#5)
11) **G Diminished 7** — G°7; G°; Gdim7; Gdim
12) **G Augmented** — G+; Gaug
13) **G Dominant 7sus4** — G7sus4, G7sus, G7add4
14) **G Major 9** — GM9; GMaj9
15) **G Dominant 7(b9)** — G7(b9); G7(−9);Gdom7(b9)
16) **G Dominant 7(#9)** — G7(#9); G7(+9); Gdom7(#9)
17) **G Minor 9** — Gm9; G-9; Gmin9; Gm7add9
18) **G Minor 6** — Gm6; G-6; Gmin6

RECOMMENDED LISTENING

- John Abercrombie
- Don Armone
- Chet Atkins
- Mickey Baker
- Billy Bauer
- Jeff Beck
- George Benson
- Dicky Betts
- Lenny Breau
- Kenny Burrell
- James Burton
- Billy Butler
- Charlie Byrd
- Larry Carlton
- Al Casey
- Al Caiola
- Eric Clapton
- Larry Coryell
- Al Di Meola
- Joe Diorio
- Herb Ellis
- Ron Eschete
- Kevin Eurbank
- Tal Farlow
- Eric Gale
- Jim Hall
- Allan Holdsworth
- John Lee Hooker
- Stanley Jordan
- Barney Kessel
- Albert King
- B.B. King
- Earl Klugh
- Mundell Lowe
- Pat Martino
- John McLaughlin
- Pat Metheny
- Tony Mottola
- Joe Pass
- Bucky Pizzarelli
- Joe Puma
- Jimmy Raney
- Lee Ritenour
- Howard Roberts
- Johnny Smith
- Toots Thieleman
- Ralph Towner
- Phil Upchurch
- George Van Eps
- Eddie Van Halen
- Muddy Waters
- Johnny Guitar Watson
- Chuck Wayne

HOW TO...

This series gives musicians the skinny on a wide variety of topics. Written by different authors with specific expertise, each title delves deep into the subject, getting readers started on the skills they're most interested in.

GUITAR BOOKS

How to Build Guitar Chops
by Chad Johnson
00147679 Book/Online Audio $16.99

How to Enjoy Guitar with Just 3 Chords
by David Harrison
00288990 Book Only.....................................$7.99

How to Fingerpick Songs on Guitar
by Chad Johnson
00155364 Book/Online Video................................$14.99

How to Get Better at Guitar
by Thorsten Kober
00157666 Book/Online Audio $19.99

How to Play Blues-Fusion Guitar
by Joe Charupakorn
00137813 Book/Online Audio $19.99

How to Play Blues/Rock Guitar Solos
by David Grissom
00249561 Book/Online Audio $16.99

How to Play Boogie Woogie Guitar
by Dave Rubin
00157974 Book/Online Video................................$14.99

How to Play Country Lead Guitar
by Jeff Adams
00131103 Book/Online Audio $19.99

How to Play Outside Guitar Licks
by Chris Buono
00140855 Book/Online Video................................$19.99

How to Play Rock Lead Guitar
by Brooke St. James
00146260 Book/Online Video................................$14.99

How to Play Rock Rhythm Guitar
by Brooke St. James
00146261 Book/Online Video................................$14.99

How to Strum Chords on Guitar
by Burgess Speed
00154902 Book/Online Video................................$14.99

BASS BOOKS

How to Create Rock Bass Lines
by Steve Gorenberg
00151784 Book/Online Audio $16.99

How to Play Blues Bass
by Mark Epstein
00260179 Book/Online Audio $14.99

DRUM BOOKS

How to Build Drum Grooves Over Bass Lines
by Alan Arber
00287564 Book/Online Audio $16.99

How to Play Rock Drums
by David Lewitt
00138541 Book/Online Audio $16.99

PIANO/KEYBOARD BOOKS

How to Play Blues Piano by Ear
by Todd Lowry
00121704 Book/Online Audio $16.99

How to Play Boogie Woogie Piano
by Arthur Migliazza & Dave Rubin
00140698 Book/Online Audio $16.99

How to Play R&B Soul Keyboards
by Henry Brewer
00232890 Book/Online Audio $16.99

How to Play Solo Jazz Piano
by John Valerio
00147731 Book/Online Audio $16.99

STRINGS BOOK

How to Play Contemporary Strings
by Julie Lyonn Lieberman
00151259 Book/Online Media....................$16.99

UKULELE BOOK

How to Play Solo Ukulele
by Chad Johnson
00159809 Book/Online Audio $16.99

VOCAL BOOK

How to Sight Sing
by Chad Johnson
00156132 Book/Online Audio $16.99

OTHER VOLUMES

How to Improvise Over Chord Changes
by Shawn Wallace, Dr. Keith Newton, Kris Johnson & Steve Kortyka
00138009 Book Only............................$24.99

How to Read Music
by Mark Phillips
00137870 Book Only.......................................$9.99

How to Record at Home on a Budget
by Chad Johnson
00131211 Book/Online Audio $19.99

How to Write Your First Song
by Dave Walker
00138010 Book/Online Audio $16.99

www.halleonard.com